MANAGEMENT IN MINUTES

Philippa Anderson

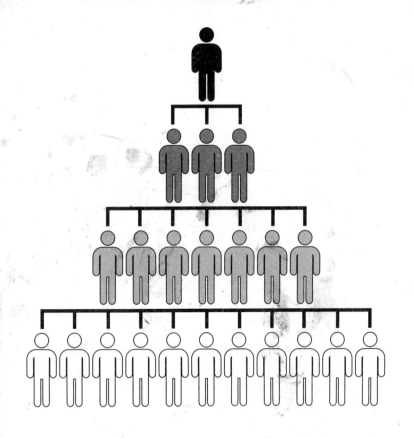

MANAGEMENT IN MINUTES

Philippa Anderson

Quercus

CONTENTS

Introduction

With rapid technological, economic and social progress, modern management is changing. This makes it both more exciting and more challenging. *Management in Minutes* takes tried and tested management concepts and makes them relevant and accessible for today.

The fundamental role of management – to make things happen through people – has not changed. But the boundaries that delineated management are eroding swiftly. What used to be a commercial, business discipline is now vital in the not-for-profit sector, too. This book is relevant to managers in all types of organizations: public, private and third sectors. Organizational boundaries are blurring with partnering, outsourcing and offshoring. Technology and the internet have created a global market, and the workplace is no longer an office; it can be home, a train, or wherever. And the work day is no longer bounded by time; people can work 24/7. These factors broaden a manager's scope and make prioritization more important than ever before.

Managers today often have to navigate through ambiguity and change. Hierarchies and formal lines of command have dissolved to flatter structures, cross-functional teams and informal networks. Rather than just employees, the composition of a manager's team can include interims, contractors and partners; and is likely to be multi-generational, diverse and virtual. 'He' and 'she' are used interchangeably in this book because a manager is just as likely to be a man or a woman.

No longer top-down, planning is dynamic and happening throughout the organization. A manager now involves people right from the outset to benefit from others' ideas, create buy-in and build the team. And managers no longer command and control. In this book we explain how managers have to empower, engage and communicate to create and maintain team cohesion and momentum.

From picking the team to managing upwards, every concept is explained succinctly here so that the essence of successful management is easily understood. We hope this book will inspire great success for established managers, aspiring managers and management students alike.

Management essentials

What is the role of a manager? Managers are needed in all types of organizations – from a small local charity to a large multi-national corporation – to use their skills, knowledge and experience to ensure that resources are organized and used efficiently and effectively to create products or services and achieve the organization's goals. All this activity happens through people, so one of the most important aspects of management is building and sustaining relationships. Getting the best from employees is vital, and exceptional managers are distinguished by the ability to coach and inspire individuals and build strong teams that deliver high performance and outstanding results. They identify and harness every employee's unique potential to deliver benefits for the individual, organization and wider stakeholders.

All this takes a mix of practical skills such as planning, soft skills such as leadership, and personal values that match the organization. An important part of a manager's role today is to model appropriate behaviours that mirror organizational culture.

Art or science?

There has long been debate about whether management is an art or a science. It can be seen as a science because of its use of scientific methods to evaluate work, develop organizational models and understand psychology. Managers can reference theories to determine the correct course of action. But general rules do not apply in every situation; theory and appropriate practice are often quite different. Managers typically consider context, draw on their experience and use their judgement. Increasingly, they need to be aware of wider issues, such as changes in society and environmental concerns, and adapt accordingly. In addition, some of the 'science' on which management principles were based is now outmoded.

Such factors see management increasingly being viewed as an art. Indeed management guru Peter Drucker describes it as a 'liberal art' – liberal because it deals with the fundamentals of leadership, knowledge from many disciplines and self-knowledge; art because it is about practical application.

Management as a discipline

The discipline of management developed out of the Industrial Revolution. New factory owners had the means of mass production, but needed to understand how to optimize output. Efforts focused on standardizing processes, utilizing labour and workflow planning. By the mid-20th century, theories abounded. Psychology was applied to workers, statistical analysis to manufacturing operations, and ergonomics to the workplace. Then came recognition that workers not only produced goods, but also created value through their use of information. The idea of the 'knowledge worker' became popular and new theories emphasized motivation and engagement.

Other ideas came from Japan, where firms ensured employees were engaged, empowered and highly productive. Concepts such as *Kaizen* (see page 332) became the vogue with an emphasis on lean production and worker involvement. Now we are in an era of accelerating change when management is less about lines of command and more about teams and networks.

Management in different sectors

Management used to be considered merely in the context of business. But no matter what type of organization – public, private or third sector – effective management is essential. The essence is to make things happen, and the starting point is the purpose of the organization, which determines what those 'things' are. The common thread is that a manager can only make things happen through people – whether it is providing healthcare services, satisfying a need for luxury cars or offering a shelter for homeless people.

A public sector organization today may not be focused on maximizing profitability, but the management challenges are just as significant as in the private sector. Faced with budget cuts, efficiency drives and massive change, similar skills need to be applied. While there is not generally a need to compete with rivals, services may be outsourced or delivered in partnership with the private sector. Equally in the third sector, resources are scarce: charities need good managers in order to do good.

'There are people who make things happen, there are people who watch things happen, and there are people who wonder what happened.'

James Lovell,
American astronaut

Management roles

Across the public, private and third sectors there are vast numbers of different management roles. Digital manager, diversity manager, insight manager, knowledge manager, social media manager – these are just some of the job titles on the internet today. New roles are emerging in response to new opportunities, and it is likely that some traditional roles will disappear. As structures become flatter, some managers will have significant people management responsibility, while others manage a few people with new specialist skills and knowledge. What does this mean for aspiring managers? Individuals are less likely to move up the rungs of an organizational ladder; sideways moves will become increasingly common. Flatter organizations have fewer layers of management, but the layers will be broader. Aspiring managers must be proactive in gaining relevant experience and developing broad skills. What will not change is that the title 'manager' will still denote responsibility for getting things done through the performance of a group of people, and interpersonal skills will continue to be vital.

shop manager diversity R&D manager HR manager
IT manager manager **knowledge manager**
healthcare manager social media manager publishing
fund-raising manager **education manager** manager
supply chain manager
customer experience manager **resourcing manager**
marketing manager organizational planning manager
station manager
customer service manager scheduling
inventory manager manager
factory manager **community manager**
purchasing manager
maintenance manager **pharmaceutical manager**
planning manager CSR manager
logistics manager quality manager
finance manager **retail manager**
digital manager airport manager
catering manager depot manager insight manager
product manager category manager

Managers and directors

The type and size of organization will influence a manager's role. A manager in a small family-owned biscuit factory could get involved in everything from sourcing raw materials to dealing with customers; while a manager in an international charity, such as UNICEF, might be a world specialist and deal only with a particular issue through a team across the globe.

Businesses can operate as sole traders, partnerships or limited companies. Every limited company has directors. A manager may also be a director and shareholder in a privately owned company. In a public company, members of the senior management team may also be executive directors, but there will also be non-executive directors who are not part of the management team, not company employees and not involved in the day-to-day running of the business. The board of directors is answerable to investor shareholders, and non-executives ensure governance, monitor executive activity and contribute to the development of strategy.

Manager vs leader

'You manage things; you lead people', according to Grace Hopper, retired US Navy admiral. At one time, management and leadership were seen as separate. The traditional view was: a manager's role is to plan, organize and coordinate what has to be done, which is an essentially skills-based job; a leader's role is to inspire and motivate, a task that requires deeper understanding of peoples' behaviour.

This may have been true in the past, but increasingly the two roles overlap. This is because people are no longer seen just as workers, but are valued for their knowledge and skills. A manager now has to organize a team of individuals not only to maximize output but also to inspire results, nurture talent and develop each person's strengths. Consider the person at the top of an organization – she cannot just do strategy and think big thoughts, she has to know what to do and how to do it. To be successful, she has to be able to balance being both a leader and a manager, using both IQ and EQ (see page 30).

Keep it simple

'If you can't explain it simply, you don't understand it well enough.' Albert Einstein knew the importance of simplicity. Too often, people in organizations overcomplicate things, thinking it makes them seem more intelligent and powerful. Business leader Jack Welch saw that managers at GE used to 'control rather than facilitate, complicate rather than simplify'.

Now genius is seen in simplicity; from clean, modern design, such as the Apple iPhone, to the move for plain language in written documents. Across organizations, people are focused on taking out complexity, but it is not just organizational structures that are being simplified: sales people now explain the benefits of products rather than their features, annual reports use diagrams rather than rows of figures, and short YouTube videos are increasingly replacing wordy instruction booklets. The manager who can solve difficult problems with simple solutions and cut through jargon and acronyms to convey a clear message is the one most likely to succeed.

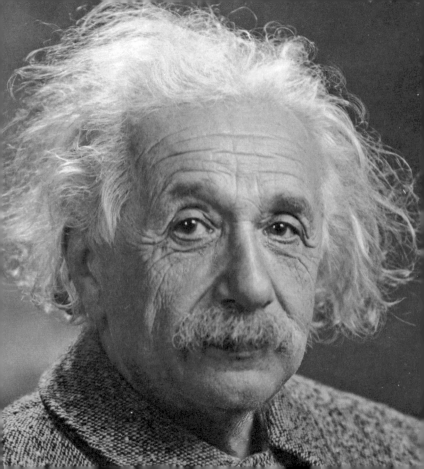

New challenges

The role of managers continues to evolve as organizations face fresh challenges in the 21st century. Many issues are around scarce resources, particularly skilled people. Managers today must compete for talent, engage and motivate individuals and teams, and work hard to retain people in the organization. Teams are becoming more diverse and multi-generational, and may include interims, contract workers or individuals working at home or overseas. Successful managers harness the strengths, knowledge and experience of every person in a team. Many are being asked to do more with less, and this can create stress – often the pressure is to satisfy key business metrics, some of which may even be contradictory. Savvy managers harness technology to achieve better management information.

The biggest overall challenge is managing through uncertainty – change can be relentless. Exceptional managers are able to lead through ambiguity and see opportunities. The following pages show common characteristics of today's outstanding managers.

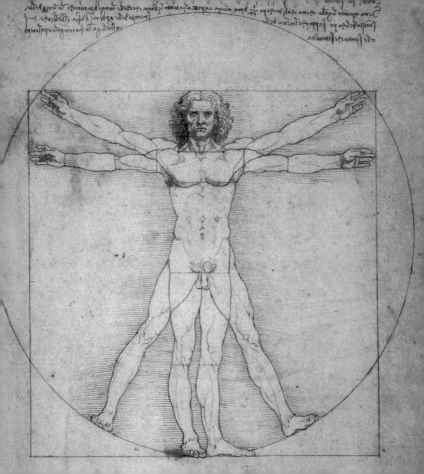

Outcome oriented

Successful managers focus on outcomes: in effect, they start at the end and work backwards. Their role is to further an organization's goal, so starting at the intended result and working out how best to utilize resources to achieve it makes good sense. The principle can be applied to any situation.

A manager might ask 'What would be a good outcome?' or 'What would success look like?' Asking such questions creates clarity around what is important – it encourages action rather than analysis. With constant change, competing agendas and complexity in many organizations, it can be easy to slide into 'analysis paralysis'. Thinking about the outcome allows a manager to be proactive rather than reactive. It helps to find a way forward and to highlight both obstacles, and ways to avoid them. Shortcuts may become apparent, too. The 80:20 rule (see page 320) may come into play. Typically other people, customers or colleagues, are also involved, so a manager might also consider what outcome *they* expect from a situation.

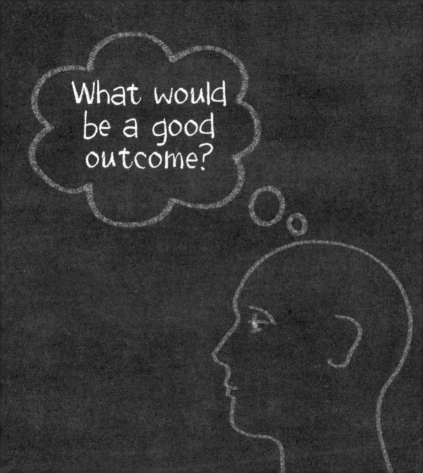

Generalist

Being a functional specialist used to be essential for taking a top management position. Now the pendulum has swung. While having a specialism is important for some organizations, many look for generalists. No matter the type of organization, managers who have broad commercial skills and knowledge are more likely to be able to make a more significant contribution. Suppose a manager with wide-ranging skills has spotted a competition threat and so needs to understand a narrow technical area of the business. He can find and employ someone with that specific technical expertise. His colleague, who has a narrow deep knowledge of a particular area, cannot simply buy in the required generalist skills and, lacking the broad perspective, may even miss the issue in the first place.

Generalists are often more adept at dealing with change because their wide knowledge makes them more adaptable. Also, evidence shows that a team of generalists performs better on a task than a team of mixed functional experts.

IQ and EQ

A high degree of intelligence, measured by the intelligence quotient (IQ) is a prerequisite for a manager because of the large scale and scope of issues and information. But organizations are concerned not only with what managers do, but also with how they do it, so they also want managers with a high degree of emotional intelligence (EQ). American psychologist Daniel Goleman, who popularized the concept, states that EQ involves several distinct competencies:

- Self-awareness: emotional awareness, knowing one's internal states, preferences, resources and intuitions
- Self-regulation: self-control, trustworthiness, adaptability; managing one's internal states, impulses and resources
- Motivation: commitment, initiative, optimism; emotional tendencies that guide or facilitate the reaching of goals
- Empathy: understanding and developing others, service orientation, leveraging diversity, political awareness
- Social skills: influence, communication, conflict management, leadership, relationship building, collaboration

	Awareness	Management
Self	Self-Awareness How am I?	Self-Management How am I managing?
Social	Social Awareness How are others?	Relationship Management How do I impact others?

Integrity

Renowned business magnate and investor Warren Buffett summarized integrity in business, saying: 'In looking for people to hire, look for three qualities: integrity, intelligence, and energy. And if they don't have the first one, the other two will kill you.'

Everyone wants to work with people they can trust. A manager known for integrity is more likely to have a loyal following and will inspire honesty in others. Integrity cannot be switched on and of: it is something that a manager has to live and breathe every day. Trust takes years to earn, but can be lost in seconds. A manager has to have his own moral compass; he has to do what he believes is right, no matter what pressure he is under and whether someone is watching or not. It may be tempting occasionally to let something go because of circumstances, or he may work in an organization where the occasional cut corner is overlooked, so long as the results come in. But people without integrity eventually get found out.

Team leader

A successful manager has to be someone that people want to follow. People look to a team leader because they feel that person helps them to do better work. A brilliant manager empowers people with a sense of 'can do' rather than restraint.

People want to respect their leader. Partly this is about seeing the leader as an example, from her working style to the way she handles relationships. But it is also about seeing evidence of outstanding decision-making ability. The decisions she makes shape the team's success and can also make or break an individual's career. People want a team leader they can see and talk to and, importantly, one who listens. Managers no longer sit behind a closed door but now have to be out at the front of the action. A strong team leader fights the battles on behalf of the team and invariably wins. She has an ability to bring the team together so that as a cohesive unit they can achieve more than if they worked individually.

Decisive

Question: 'Would you say you are decisive?' Answer: 'I'm not sure.' It is an age-old joke but one that has serious implications in any organization. The pace of business is so fast today that managers have to make decisions promptly so the team has clear direction and does not lose momentum. An inherent fear of making mistakes is one of the most common reasons for risk aversion or the inability to take decisions. There is often no right answer (see page 244) and a manager is unlikely to ever have all the information. He just has to decide!

Some sit on the fence, or get caught up in overanalysis. Suppose a manager can't make a decision – he may buy time by announcing that further competitor analysis is vital to the decision-making process. The team sees this pointless information gathering as procrastination and soon the manager has a reputation for being indecisive. This can lead to frustration among the team and loss of credibility with team members and colleagues alike.

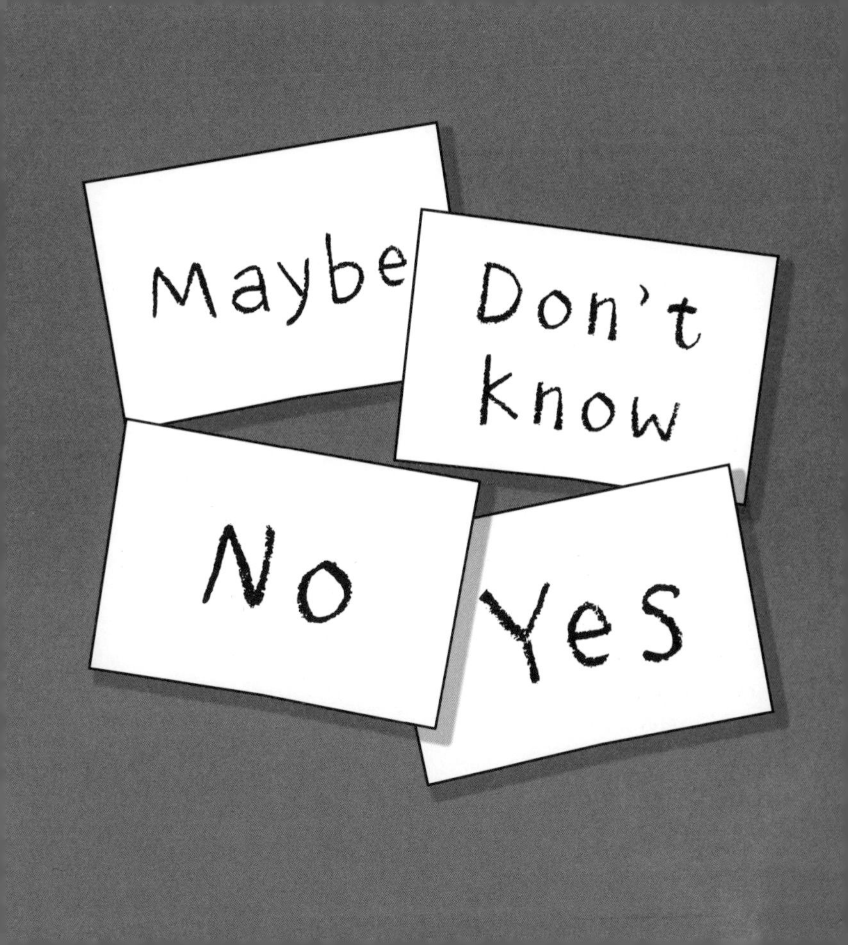
Maybe
Don't know
No
Yes

Future thinker

'If you see a bandwagon, it's too late' – that was the view of successful businessman James Goldsmith. If a manager is overly concerned with short-term results, he will neglect the future. The story of how Kodak executives reaped the profits of film-processing while ignoring the approaching digital market is well known. On the other hand, indifference to the short term will put the future in jeopardy.

A skilled manager is able to keep an eye both on today, and on the shifting horizon. He may allocate specific time to consider the future beyond immediate priorities. This gets him out of the business-as-usual mindset, and allows him to consider things such as market changes, emerging trends and competition. Some organizations set up forums for future thinking as a way to help managers generate ideas to give the firm a competitive edge. Future thinking is not a simple linear process: it requires managers to develop ways to spot what's happening, to join the dots to see patterns and trends, and to identify opportunities.

Seeing the big picture – and the detail

Managers who can see the big picture are visionary and strategic. They can devise a high-level plan for the organization, think broadly and understand how everything fits together. They are often described as right-brained: creative and able to see patterns in complex problems. A detail manager focuses narrowly on specific aspects of the organization, often misses the wider picture and tends to be more tactical. They are often described as left-brained: logical, analytical thinkers.

These two distinctive types of manager can complement each other because each has a different skill set, and while typically people are naturally more skilled in one area, the ideal manager spans both. He can visualize the big picture, but also drill down to ensure the business does not come unstuck because of lack of attention to operational detail. Shifting from being high up with a bird's eye view, to being on the ground and immersed in the execution of a plan is not an easy transition, but is a capability that can be acquired with training and development.

Firefighting

Good managers are proactive and use effective risk management to spot and prevent potential disasters (see page 246). But every manager has to be ready and able to step into a crisis. Daily difficulties come in many guises. It may be a problem with a manufacturing line, a quality issue or a physical problem such as a flooded building. And it might have an impact that affects the company's operation, customers or reputation. A good manager stays calm – she is the one everyone looks to for a decision. The natural response would be to start reacting, but she has to establish the facts, understand the scale and implications, and then determine the action. It may be something that can be resolved simply or it may have to involve a crisis management team.

How an organization's leader responds to a crisis can make matters worse. The 2010 BP disaster in the Gulf of Mexico is a prime example. With today's global media, organizations have to ensure their managers are equipped to deal with anything.

Constant learning

Good managers are sponges; they continually absorb learning. It is not simply that the world and workplace are changing rapidly, learning is vital for individuals to develop and grow. The moment a manager thinks he knows it all, he becomes complacent and falls behind.

Thousands of business, management and self-help books are published each year. But wisdom is not just facts and figures, it is about learning from people. This means getting out from behind the desk and being curious. A manager intent on learning has to ask open questions and listen (see page 258). He should get to know people in his business, network with peers in other organizations and attend conferences on his subject matter or wider topics. Mistakes are also a great way to learn, and he should ensure that project reviews cover both what did, and what *did not* work. An effective manager keeps a journal of vital information and key learning; the act of writing something down focuses attention and makes it memorable.

Entrepreneurs

A great manager thinks like an entrepreneur; he has passion, always looks for a better option and derives personal satisfaction from what he does. Think of entrepreneurs like James Dyson, Richard Branson (Virgin) and Jeff Bezos (Amazon). What do they have in common? They believe in what they do, take it seriously but still have fun, and work tirelessly in pursuit of their goal. Their products and services have a reputation that is hard to beat. They are shameless self-promoters, taking every opportunity to talk positively about their brand and products. The customer is always at the forefront of their minds. They use technology and processes to give them a competitive edge. Making connections and seeing opportunities is just how they think. They know that with every action comes risk and, because they started with limited means, they know that wise use of resources, including cash, is vital. Broader industry issues interest them and they speak out. Perhaps most of all they are creative and inspirational. Who would not want to work for a manager like that?

Organizations

Watch children playing and they will soon start to organize themselves, with one or more taking a leadership role as they begin to form a structure. Organizations need structure because people and tasks need some form of order. An organization chart (or organogram) can show formal relationships between different areas and ranking of roles. Structure could be based on function, geographic region, service, product or product group, or customers. Some organizations also develop informal structures (see page 134).

The character and culture of an organization is often reflected in its structure. Traditional organizations, such as the National Health Service (NHS) in the UK, are likely to have a hierarchical structure and bureaucratic culture. Younger ones, such as Google, are more likely to have flat structures and highly collaborative cultures. Structures in long-established organizations may no longer be fit for purpose – some may undertake restructuring in an attempt to change their culture.

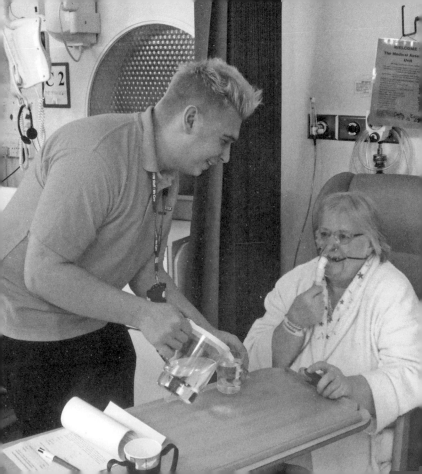

Hierarchies vs flat structures

The traditional way of structuring an organization is a hierarchy based on reporting levels. This has some advantages: roles are clear and the structure enables work to flow down through the organization so things run smoothly. Typically it involves three levels of management: junior managers, involved in day-to-day issues and responsible for non-management employees; middle managers, often general managers who are involved in operations but rely on input from first-level managers; and senior managers, typically the top executives responsible for strategy and direction.

The disadvantage of a hierarchy is that its layers can form barriers to progress and growth; opportunities for cooperation may be missed. Elimination of some management positions can result in cost savings and a flatter structure. People tend to feel more involved and motivated because there is improved communication and less feeling of bureaucracy. A flat structure is more often found in small organizations.

Hierarchy

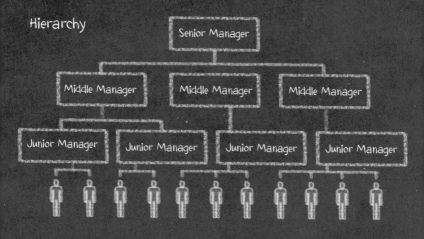

Flat structures

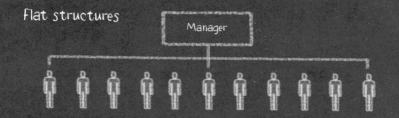

Matrix structure

Matrix structures occur in large companies with different products or services across the globe, or where cross-functional teams are set up for a project. An organization is set up as a grid or matrix, typically with an upward reporting line to a functional manager and a horizontal line to another manager, such as a business or project manager. People are deployed to share skills across areas or projects, information flows both across and through the organization, and motivation and decision-making can be enhanced through strong teams.

Despite these benefits, working in a matrix structure can be tough. It can be difficult to coordinate and balance workloads, people's loyalties may be divided and formal authority can be unclear. It is a particular challenge for a manager whose team has dual reporting relationships. He has to ensure that people have clear roles and responsibilities and understand the team's objectives and KPIs (see page 402). Regular communication with the team and peer managers helps avoid misunderstandings.

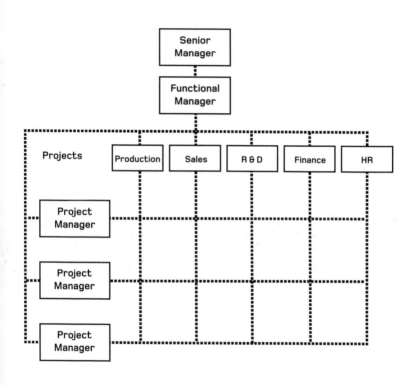

Functions

Many organizations arrange work by function. Each function or department, typically headed by a manager, is responsible for a particular specialism or area. This provides clarity about where responsibilities lie. Essential functions in most organizations include finance, human resources and information technology. These provide services across the business and enable its operation. Part or all of these functions may be outsourced, but in some of these functions, particularly finance, a manager may also be a director sitting on the board.

Additional functions, such as purchasing, distribution and customer services, will depend on the line of business. For example, most charities have a fund-raising department to generate income, while a consumer goods company may have a large marketing department. The most important function is often the one responsible for the core business. In a food manufacturing company, for example, production is the heart of the operation, as it generates the products to sell.

Projects and programmes

A traditional functional structure is not always the best way to organize work, particularly if the work does not fit into business as usual. Where there is a discrete goal, firms may set up a project, or cross-functional team, that brings together expertise from different areas of the business. Suppose a company is considering buying a firm that makes compatible products. It could set up a temporary team and allocate specialists from areas such as finance, marketing and HR (and possibly external consultants). The team would consider the viability, develop a strategy for the acquisition and plan integration of the new and existing businesses. Once the project was complete, the team could then be dissolved and its people moved back to a functional role or to another project.

Organizations also set up longer-term programmes. These typically involve a number of inter-related projects that are coordinated under an umbrella programme to achieve a broad goal for the organization, such as improving profitability.

Project 1: Reduce manufacturing costs

Project 2: Improve customer service

Project 3: Improve quality

Project 4: Improve customer payments

Project 5: Increase speed to market

Project 6: Improve supplier terms

} PROFITABILITY PROGRAMME

Business units

Large organizations are often split into business units. Typically each business unit (BU), or strategic business unit (SBU), will operate as an autonomous organization with a specific focus on a product line, and will be of sufficient size to have its own functions such as finance and HR. AngloAmerican, for example, is a global, diversified mining business with eight BUs based on different minerals including iron ore, copper, platinum and diamonds. Each operates around the globe, is headed by a CEO and has its own vision and strategy.

Global giant GE pioneered the concept of strategic business units in the 1970s; today its SBUs span aviation to healthcare. The organization had become too big to operate under a traditional pyramid structure and its different assets were involved in diverse markets requiring different strategies. Although a manager working in a large organization with numerous SBUs may feel he is a small fish in a large pond, there are benefits, such as opportunities for networking and career advancement within the organization.

Department structure

A manager has to organize the work for his own area or department, which involves the creation of a structural framework of duties and responsibilities. The following steps are typical of an effective manager's approach:

- Determine the objectives – what needs to be achieved?
- Consider the activities – what must be done to achieve each objective?
- Determine roles – assign activities to individuals so there is clear responsibility and no duplication or overlap.
- Select individuals for the roles – find the right person with the right skills for the right job.
- Assign authority – give individuals power to take decisions, coach individuals and manage subordinates.
- Provide physical environment and tools – ensure an effective working environment.
- Synchronize activities – coordinate activities and efforts.
- Communicate regularly – consistent communication keeps people involved and reinforces structure.

Span of control

The term 'span of control' refers to the number of employees that report directly to a manager. A narrow span of control is where a manager has few direct reports and a wide span is where a larger number of people report directly to him. It is an important concept because it affects fixed labour costs, reporting relationships and information flow, and decision-making speeds – major considerations in organization design.

For example, narrow spans typically mean more managers and more layers (i.e. a more hierarchical and bureaucratic organization). The general trend is to eliminate unnecessary positions and move to wider spans of management. So is there an optimum span of control? Various factors are still likely to have an influence, including the capability of managers and subordinates, job complexity and physical location. According to *The Economist*, six direct reports was typical in the early 20th century, but numbers have increased – American multinational GE now has a guideline of 10-15 people reporting to one person.

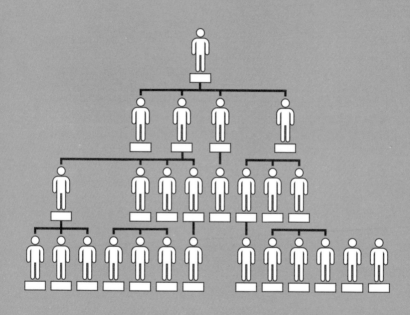

Virtual organizations

The meaning of a virtual organization varies – it may be one where employees are geographically dispersed and linked by a shared computer system, or one with a handful of employees, where traditional functions are outsourced. The common theme is that an organization appears to have more capability than it actually has. Hollywood is often given as an example: unconnected people coming together with a shared purpose to make a particular film.

Boundaries in such organizations are indistinct. Internal and external alliances are fluid and depend on who can get the job done in the shortest time. Responsibilities will move accordingly. Managers therefore need a different skill set from those needed in a traditional hierarchy. Learning, for example, is altered as there is no corporate memory and more reliance on networks of knowledge. Flexibility, coping with ambiguity, an ability to motivate virtual teams and an aptitude for creating external virtual relationships are some of the emerging skills.

Organizational culture

Every organization has its own distinct culture – a complex mix of the norms, values and behaviours within it. Culture is often a reflection of the type of organization. For example, an innovative business such as Google is more likely to have an open, creative culture, while a cancer charity is more likely to have a culture focused on compassion and care. Culture is often described as the glue that holds the organization together, or simply 'how we do things'. This can be written down (often in glossy mission statements), but it is people – particularly the managers – who help shape the culture and make it real. The actions of senior people set the pattern, so if the overall leader tends to use a bullying style this will be perpetuated through the organization.

A manager who is new to an organization may think that the written rules are the best guideline, but often the reality is far more complex. She will have to observe and listen to pick up the nuances.

Strategy

Strategy is the way that an organization gets from where it is now, to where it wants to be. But it is more than just a long-term plan: it is the direction set by an organization's executives to achieve the best outcome, with all possible obstacles considered and understood. Strategy has to start with information and analysis. There are different methods to help structure this thinking, such as SWOT (where strengths, weaknesses, opportunities and threats are analysed – see page 338). Successful strategy development involves people across the organization, because they are best placed to have information about customers, competitors and markets. This also builds commitment – people understand the direction because they have been involved in the thinking. Good strategies are clear on scope; they include products a company will and will not make, and the markets it should or should not compete in. But devising a robust strategy is one thing, and successful execution is another: some managers fail to deliver on the firm's strategy, or fail to adapt when situations change.

Direction to get
best outcome

Context

A firm's executives would be unlikely to decide on selling ice cream to increase sales if the business was based in a cold-climate country. Successful managers understand the importance of the operating environment as this provides the context. Information about the market, customers and competitors is vital to shape decisions on strategy.

The first step in devising successful strategy is to get accurate information and make sense of the facts. Suppose a firm is considering opening a new store in a certain town. The team involved will need to research and discover information on: other stores in the town, how many people visit, public transport links, any plans for new housing developments, etc. Only then can the manager and his team move to the second stage of making a decision, and the third stage of implementation. An effective manager thinks about context in every situation: he gathers information and builds a picture of the operating environment. No manager can work in a vacuum.

Purpose, mission and vision

When President Kennedy visited NASA during the Apollo moon programme of the 1960s he asked a man carrying a broom about his job. Legend has it the man replied: 'I'm helping to put a man on the moon.' People need to understand an organization's purpose to have a reason to go through the door and work, and to provide a framework for their role.

A purpose statement explains *why* an organization exists, and is the foundation and reference point for all the organization's activities. What the organization does to accomplish that purpose is often explained in a mission statement. This is the way the purpose becomes real: it may include more detail and so provide focus for the organization's activities – for example, articulating customer type, geographic priorities or service levels. Some organizations have a vision statement, too. The vision is where the business or charity will be in a number of years' time if it achieves its purpose. It is the long-term goal, and often includes a measurable impact.

Objectives and goals

While strategy defines an overall direction, goals are the achievement towards which the effort is aimed, and business objectives are statements of what will be achieved in a given period of time. In practice, the words goal and objective are often used interchangeably, even though an objective is a measurable target that must be achieved to reach a goal.

Objectives are set at an organizational level first. A business, for example, may have an objective of increasing sales by 10 per cent in a year, while a charity for the homeless may have an objective of providing shelter for 10 per cent more people during the year. Clear organizational objectives are necessary because it helps people to focus on a shared aim. Achievement of objectives is important as it marks progress towards the main goal. Team and individual objectives must align with those of the organization to ensure everyone is focused in the same direction. Managers should be clear on their own goals - things they want to achieve – and their objectives, or specific targets.

SMART objectives

A simple, effective and proven way to set objectives is to use the well-known acronym SMART. This stands for:

- Specific: what is to be achieved (e.g. increased profits)
- Measurable: the desired outcome stated as a number that can be measured, (e.g. increase profits by 10 per cent)
- Achievable: so that people buy into achieving the objective, it must be achievable, not aspirational
- Relevant: the objective is relevant given factors such as market conditions, available skills and financial resources
- Timely: a clear timeframe for the objective so that people are clear when it should be achieved (e.g. 12 months).

Suppose an organization sets an objective to increase online sales by 40 per cent by 31 December. Each manager takes this objective and agrees team and individual objectives. The digital manager, for example, may agree with her team to improve search engine optimization by 80 per cent by 30 June. She can then work with team members to set individual objectives.

S - Specific

M - Measurable

A - Agreed and achievable

R - Relevant

T - Timely

Values

How a manager does his job, for example the way he treats people, is just as important as what he achieves. Many organizations have explicit values that determine rules of behaviour and guide business decisions and actions. More than statements on paper, values provide a moral compass for an organization and its employees. Organizations damage both reputation and shareholder value if they claim to have values such as honesty or trust but are then involved in lawsuits for bribery. Likewise a manager has to live the organization's values because people follow what he does, more than what he says.

'What gets measured gets done; what gets rewarded gets repeated,' according to one pizza company CEO, and so it is with values. Increasingly, organizations are aligning their values with their reward and incentive schemes. They are also seeking to recruit and develop people who match their values from the outset, recognizing that it is important to select people who inherently hold similar beliefs as values cannot be imposed.

Stakeholders

Every organization and department has stakeholders – these can be individuals, groups or other organizations, and they can be internal or external. Stakeholders are likely to have diverse, even conflicting, interests, and any decision taken by a manager can affect those interests. Primary stakeholders are those with the biggest stake in a business, such as shareholders, employees and customers, but increasingly local communities are also seen as stakeholders.

The more decisions a manager takes, the more people she will impact. No manager is going to be able to keep every stakeholder happy, but what she can do is identify them, prioritize them and then manage them according to what she needs to achieve. A large part of this is managing expectations, which involves developing an understanding of stakeholders' interests and motivation so that their support can be won. This can range from full involvement in a project to simply keeping a group or individual informed.

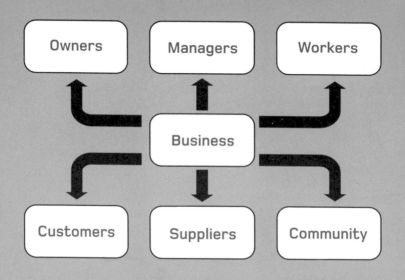

Corporate social responsibility

In the 1970s, US economist Milton Friedman famously said: 'The social responsibility of business is to make a profit.' And for some time the main focus for firms was merely financial, until it was recognized that organizations should be ethical and not harm people, local communities or the environment. Today, many companies look to go beyond this in a genuine commitment to help build a better society. This corporate social responsibility (CSR) has to be integral to the way a company runs its operation, rather than a separate consideration, so brings benefits in terms of corporate reputation and attracts employees and customers. It includes sourcing raw materials from ethical suppliers, supporting local communities with health and education, and considering product design, production and disposal to minimize environmental impact.

CSR is implicit in a good strategy. An effective manager is guided by social responsibility in day-to-day decisions, from selecting a new supplier to making a decision on a project.

SOCIETAL RESPONSIBILITY
Support community; Improve quality of life

ENVIRONMENTAL RESPONSIBILITY
Do no harm to environment, be sustainable

ETHICAL RESPONSIBILITY
Do what is right/moral

LEGAL RESPONSIBILITY
Comply with law

ECONOMIC RESPONSIBILITY
Be profitable; financially viable

CORPORATE SOCIAL RESPONSIBILITY

Sustainability

When New College Oxford found that the beams in its historic dining hall had beetle infestation, fresh oak was readily available for replacement. The hall had been built in the late 14th century, and the story goes that oak saplings had been planted with great foresight by foresters of the time. The concept of sustainability is not new, but such considerations have come to the fore with a growing world population, climate change concerns and pressure on global resources.

Managers have to understand the risks and opportunities associated with the firm's environmental and social impacts: key issues include industrial waste, use of water and scarce resources, sustainable development of raw materials, emissions and community development. Many organizations have processes, frameworks and measurement tools in place to support managers in these matters. Unilever, for example, sets targets and metrics for managers, including total water consumption and greenhouse-gas emissions.

Customers

Without customers, a business does not exist. Every firm has to be able to answer the question: 'Who are my customers?' Firms can have more than one customer – for example with retailers as the middle man between them and the consumer. This is changing as the digital economy now enables consumers to interact directly with a firm via multiple channels. And with growing choice and global interconnectivity, consumers are increasingly discerning, demanding and vocal.

Management guru Peter Drucker first introduced the idea of delivering customer value in the 1970s, when he explained that a customer 'buys the satisfaction of a want'. This value is a complex mix of economic, emotional and psychological considerations, affected by the media and now the internet. One person's perception of quality, for example, may be totally different from another's. In addition to understanding a firm's external customers, managers in certain departments need to recognize internal customers elsewhere in the organization.

Customer satisfaction

'There is only one boss: the customer. And he can fire everybody in the company, from the chairman on down, simply by spending his money somewhere else.' That's the view of US businessman Sam Walton – and as the founder of the world's biggest retailer Walmart, he should know.

Customer satisfaction is vital in our modern environment of global competition, where anything is available anywhere at the click of a mouse, and feedback is often broadcast over the internet where anyone can see it. Companies invest millions of pounds in customer relationships and surveys. For example, high-end car companies such as Mercedes-Benz have a large customer service team to ensure an ongoing relationship with the customer and encourage repeat purchases. Many organizations liken the sustaining of this relationship as encouraging the customer to move up a ladder of commitment from sales prospect through regular customer to an ardent advocate.

Advocate – loyal customer who actively recommends organization to others.

Client – person who buys regularly and supports the organization, but is passive

Regular customer – person who buys regularly but is neutral towards organization

One-off purchaser – person who has bought just once

Prospect – person might be persuaded to buy

Products

A product has to satisfy a consumer need and make a profit for the business. The need is the starting point that sparks an initial idea, and the manufactured product then progresses through a product life cycle. That is the traditional concept, but technology is challenging this. Many best-selling products today, such as the Apple iPad, succeed by pioneering categories where most people did not even perceive a need.

The way firms manufacture products is changing, too. America used to be the unquestioned manufacturing leader, before Germany and Japan started to compete. The idea of outsourcing (where a firm pays someone else to produce goods) and offshoring (where a firm moves production abroad) came along. China and other industrializing nations led the way in low-cost production. Now, there is a move to bring manufacturing back to domestic markets to ensure speed to customers. Innovation, not only in products but also in how they are made and brought to market, is vital in a rapidly changing world.

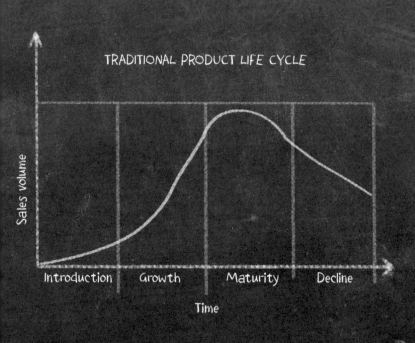

Services

As people's income rises and they have satisfied material needs, they begin to demand more services or 'intangible' goods. These may include both long-established services such as government, health and education, and relatively new ones, such as communications, information and business services. In the UK, for example, the service sector now accounts for three-quarters of the economy, and includes hotels, bars, restaurants, hairdressers, IT and transport.

Producing services rather than goods requires fewer natural or physical resources, but more human resources. So the emphasis for managers is even more on recruiting people with the right skills. For business and financial services, more educated workers are required, while frontline roles in hotels, restaurants and cafés rely more on social rather than technical skills. Service companies have many ways to differentiate themselves with customers, including loyalty programmes and regular communications.

Resources

Every manager needs to secure the right resources to do the job, and to manage those resources efficiently. These may include materials, people and finance. Managers are in competition with others in their own organization for resources, especially the best people: an astute manager is aware of this and uses influencing skills to acquire a talented team. She also ensures that when the annual budgeting cycle comes round she has accurate data and a robust case to justify her resources.

Increasing competition means continuous pressure on managing costs, and managers are often asked to use resources more efficiently. Cost cutting might mean having to ask suppliers to reduce their costs, getting rid of contractors or not being allowed to replace permanent staff who leave. Physical materials are always under review, as holding stock is costly – raw materials and finished goods take space and could become obsolete. Managers may look at ways to bring inventory costs down, such as only manufacturing goods to order.

Marketing

Marketing is the way firms anticipate, identify and satisfy customer needs. It is a mix of the right product, at the right price, in the right place, using the most effective promotion. These 'Four Ps' were first used by US marketer E. Jerome McCarthy in 1960, and are still widely used today:

- Product – features and appearance of goods and services, includes quality, design, packaging, guarantees and support
- Price – the price a consumer is prepared to pay for the goods or services, which influences profit, includes discounting and credit options
- Place – distribution and retail and online channels, includes business location, shop front, logistics
- Promotion – how the benefits of the product or service are communicated, includes advertising, point-of-sale promotions, direct selling and publicity.

For many firms, one or more of the elements in this mix will be more relevant, depending on the product or service, as shown opposite.

PRODUCT/SECTOR		RELEVANCE
Luxury cars Designer furniture	→	Product
Supermarkets Low-cost airline	→	Price
Convenience store Coffee shop	→	Place
Fast-Moving Consumer Goods Low-cost holidays	→	Promotion

Selling

Selling is often viewed negatively, perhaps thanks to high-pressure techniques used in certain areas. Yet trading and selling is the basis of all business, and the skills are important for all, not just for customer-facing managers. Whatever the organization, managers will use selling techniques in daily activities, whether presenting a new project to the board for approval or attracting a potential employee. Organizations recognize this, and often include a sales role in their graduate or commercial training programmes. Negotiation skills, for example, are linked to selling and vital in management: they include the ability to listen, evaluate possibilities, identify key stakeholders, deal with objections or conflicting opinions, and ultimately reach an agreement that suits both parties.

Selling varies across sectors. Differentiated products and services are essential in the highly competitive consumer marketplace, while business-to-business selling is far more about partnership and collaboration to benefit both parties.

Brands

'Products are made in the factory, but brands are created in the mind,' said advertising mogul Walter Landor. Buy a Big Mac without the brand and it is just a burger. Consumers see brands such as McDonald's or Coca-Cola and know what they stand for. A brand is more than just a logo: it is created by different elements, including language, imagery, associations and values. A business can differentiate its products, appeal to distinct consumer groups and grow customer loyalty with its brands, and branding can also be important for non-profit organizations such as charities.

Employer branding has become important since the 1990s: it applies marketing principles to people management, and is a way for organizations to differentiate themselves in the labour market. It is an important concept, not least because brands are a major part of modern life. The employer brand reflects the consumer brand personality; Facebook, say, offers a very different work experience to working at an international bank.

Unique selling proposition

A unique selling proposition (USP) is the thing that makes an organization or a product stand out. The uniqueness might be, for example: the best quality, best price, quickest service, most choice, least calories, locally sourced ingredients or extended warranty. A firm has to know its customers and understand the problems they face: the proposition explains why a firm can solve the customer's problem better than any other firm, and so why the customer should choose them.

Toiletries brand Dove, part of Unilever, stands out from other brands because, through research, it recognized that women worry about self-image. Dove came up with a USP to overcome this problem: Dove does not want to change customers with cosmetics, but to support their real beauty. Dove launched a 'campaign for real beauty' to celebrate individuality, features women of all shapes, sizes and ages in advertisements rather than stereotypical models, and uses slogans such as: 'Imagine a world in which beauty is a source of confidence, not anxiety'.

Quality

People know quality when they see it. Typically, the higher the price a consumer pays, the higher the quality they expect. Firms manage quality by setting standards and checking, for example, when raw materials arrive in the factory, during production and before despatch of the finished goods. Equally, managers are responsible for the quality of work leaving their department: for example, a manager may ask to see the slides before a major presentation to ensure its content is clear.

Total quality management (TQM) is a much wider concept. It is a strategic and systematic approach that puts quality at the heart of an organization's activities and culture. The organization is viewed as a series of horizontal processes that take inputs from suppliers through to outputs delivered to the customer. The focus is on managing and improving processes rather than outcomes. Effective communication to maintain momentum, the right working environment and a focus on common goals are important for managers involved in TQM.

Supply chain

Supplying quality, timely and effective products and services to customers is the aim of every business. Supply chain management is the way a company manages its resources along the journey to meet that demand. Firms generally have an overall plan that incorporates key metrics to ensure their supply chains are efficient and effective. This might, for example, involve activities being outsourced to another firm, being undertaken by an offshore branch, or include working with external suppliers to optimize stock levels. Supply chain includes logistics: once considered a backroom function, it is increasingly important in a competitive market because it includes how the company fulfils customer orders. With online businesses in particular, delivery is part of the customer experience. Supply chain also has to include an efficient system for dealing with goods returned by the consumer. Rather than looking at the supply chain as merely a series of activities, some organizations look at how value is created at each stage of the process (see page 328).

People

Many annual reports used to feature the cliché 'people are our greatest asset' but the phrase has been subject to much debate and has lost credibility. People are not an asset on the balance sheet, yet the underlying meaning of the phrase is true. Without the effort and commitment of employees an organization can achieve nothing. Henry Ford recognized this when he said: 'You can take my factories, burn up my buildings, but give me my people and I'll build the business right back again.'

It is said that people don't leave organizations, they leave managers. Establishing a robust relationship with each employee is fundamental for a good manager. People are the most important aspect of a manager's job but can also provide the most challenges. A manager has to find the right people, get to know them as individuals, understand what motivates them, coach them and evaluate and reward their performance. He also needs the ability to discipline a member of his team, make a person redundant or fire someone.

Selection

Before a manager thinks about selection, she needs to work out the sort of person needed for a job. Defining these requirements at the outset helps ensure the right person for the role. It also ensures there is a real job to do: often it can become clear that recruitment is unnecessary because the work is temporary or can be combined with another role.

She starts by writing a job description that sets out the purpose of the job, the responsibilities and accountabilities, general duties and where the job fits in the organization structure. A person specification is also needed, which lists the qualifications, skills, experience and personal attributes required. Many managers also specify competencies (see page 120) that help determine whether the individual will fit with the organization's culture. A thorough screening of applications, ideally with the help of HR, is vital to ensure the manager does not waste time interviewing candidates who do not match the must-have list on the person specification.

MUST HAVE

Science degree

Five years' work experience

Second language – French

Knowledge of health service

The interview

Thorough screening of applications should ensure a manager only sees candidates that meet the essential criteria for a job. The interview should then be the opportunity to determine whether candidates demonstrate the desired competencies.

Preparation is important to ensure the interview is objective. Ideally the manager, with HR colleagues, should agree and ask consistent, open-ended questions. For example: 'Describe a situation where you had to work under pressure.' Using the same questions for each candidate helps distinguish the person who best matches the criteria for the role. An 80:20 rule applies; the candidate should do 80 per cent of the talking and the manager or HR person only 20 per cent. Part of the interview is selling the job to candidates, so a smooth interview process and prompt follow-up helps create a favourable impression. Laws on discrimination can be a minefield, so a manager can only ask questions related directly to the job. If in doubt, he should get expert advice before the interview.

Diversity

The shift to a more diverse workforce is a reflection of increasing globalization and a more open society. Profit and non-profit organizations now recognize that a diverse workforce brings benefits including creativity, unexplored opportunities and willingness to change. 'Strength lies in differences, not in similarities,' according to author Stephen Covey.

Managing diversity is more than simply acknowledging differences; it involves recognizing the value of differences and encouraging inclusiveness. Organizations have to have processes and practices in place to ensure a fair environment where everyone has access to equal opportunities. Training and communication may be needed to reinforce appropriate behaviours. Managers have to understand company principles and the law. Avoiding discrimination on any grounds is crucial. A manager has to be aware of any personal biases and be particularly wary of wanting to recruit people who are similar to him; merit must always be the yardstick.

Performance management

Many organizations have some form of performance management process to set out what is expected of employees, facilitate support and provide a framework for performance to be measured. A good system should be part of a culture where people take responsibility for their own continuous improvement, and supports the development of strong relationships between a manager and his team.

The process starts with planning. The manager works with the employee to agree individual objectives, aligned to business plans and organizational objectives. Progress against these objectives is reviewed regularly, and usually once a year in a performance appraisal (see page 118). It is a continuous process with objectives reassessed and adjusted if required. Many organizations have shifted away from measuring individual output linked to pay increases, to focusing on contribution to organizational objectives through behaviour and capabilities, often defined in organizational competencies.

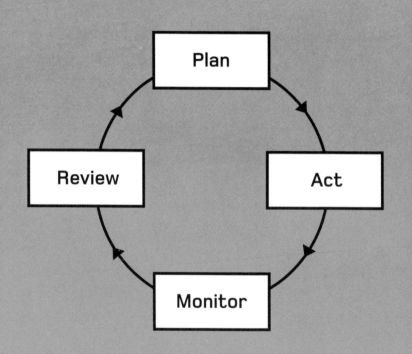

Performance appraisals

The appraisal is part of a process; preparation by both manager and employee is necessary for it to be beneficial to both sides. The manager must gather relevant information on the individual's progress against objectives and performance against competencies, as well as notes from previous appraisals.

There is no right or wrong way to conduct an appraisal. Much depends on the employee, the business and the degree of formality. Ideally, an informal approach eases the conversation and covers the essential elements: performance against agreed objectives, behaviour against values or competencies, feedback on progress, constructive comments, open discussion including employee expectations and needs, and joint agreement on next steps. An effective manager will ensure that he listens actively, allows time for reflection, focuses on performance and behaviour rather than the individual's personality, looks at the whole time period rather than isolated or recent events and ends the meeting positively with agreed plans of action.

	Poor	Excellent
Quality of work	☐	☐
Quantity of work	☐	☐
Initiative	☐	☐
Adaptability	☐	☐
Cooperation	☐	☐
Dependability	☐	☐
Communication skills	☐	☐
Supervision	☐	☐
Versatility	☐	☐
Relations	☐	☐
Leadership skills	☐	☐

Competencies

Few organizations tolerate people who deliver brilliant results but have an abusive manner. Employers recognize that effective performance in a job requires a mix of skills, behaviour and attitude. Competencies, incorporating different aspects of these elements, are developed by many organizations as the indicator of what employees need to match the organization's culture. They are used in recruitment, performance management and to support training and development. Organizations create a competency framework, with measures for different levels of seniority. Typically there are no more than 12 competencies, and different roles in the organization may place more emphasis on particular ones.

Distinguishing between what must be achieved by an individual (i.e. objectives) and how things are done (i.e. competencies) is important for any manager. A well-defined set of behaviours provides clarity and consistency for the manager when dealing with employees and helps avoid subjectivity.

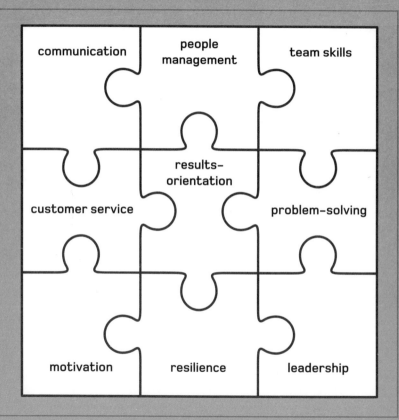

Giving feedback

One recommended way to give feedback is the sandwich method – say something nice at the beginning and end, with constructive feedback in the middle. Others believe that getting straight to the point with a clear aim of helping the individual understand the impact of their actions or behaviour can be more effective. Whatever method, a manager needs to have evidence or examples to hand and should always base feedback on facts, not her subjective opinion. An effective way to give feedback is for her to describe an event and encourage the individual to come to their own conclusion. For example, she might say: 'You always contribute a lot during team meetings and make some good points; do you think it may prevent others from getting their views across?' Rather than saying: 'You talk too much in meetings.' The emphasis should always be on putting it right next time rather than criticism. When something has gone wrong, the employee should be given the opportunity to suggest ways of correcting the situation rather than the manager directing what should happen.

Reward and recognition

Reward is the compensation package for doing a particular job, which may include pay and benefits such as paid holidays, pension contributions and childcare vouchers. These rewards are external to the individual, and so are referred to as extrinsic factors. Reward is transactional, impersonal and rarely a motivator. Recognition is different because it influences how a person feels inside: intrinsic motivation. Being recognized for an achievement can give a psychological boost that is likely to be remembered long after a bonus cheque is spent.

Every manager has a key role to play in recognition. Aside from formal programmes, such as employee of the month, he can recognize individuals in random, unexpected ways. There are many ideas: a voucher for a meal with a partner, a bunch of flowers, an Amazon voucher, a bottle of champagne or cakes for the team. A simple, hand-written, thank-you note can mean a great deal. Aside from the feel-good factor, recognition helps reinforce positive actions, behaviours and business outcomes.

Dealing with difficult people

Different personalities, increasing workloads and changing priorities can sometimes combine to create a fraught work environment. When someone is not their best or is downright difficult it can be a challenge for a manager.

When an individual does not conform to expected standards, the first thing for a manager to establish is whether this is a one-off incident. The person could just be having a bad day and need friendly support. It may be that feedback is required (see page 122), particularly if the individual is unaware of the impact of their behaviour on others. A good manager always takes action if difficult behaviour is ongoing. He makes it clear that it is unacceptable, because he knows that if the situation is not addressed it usually gets worse. When an individual is continually problematic, it may be that they need support to organize their workload, or there may be a deeper root cause outside of work. Talking through the incident, perhaps with support from the HR team, may be helpful for all involved.

Mavericks

Some of the best ideas come from the most difficult people to manage: there are going to be mavericks in any organization. They refuse to toe the line, they take risks and have a level of confidence that can be misinterpreted as arrogance. And yet they can often deliver outstanding and original results.

The challenge for the manager of such an individual is to look for positive ways to harness their energy, while working to minimize the negative impact of their unconventional style. The maverick has to understand what they are expected to contribute to the organization. So specific goals and defined limits are essential. The manager must make it clear that the individual can choose their own route, but needs to conform to the organization's values. Mavericks often have little respect for hierarchy, and so the manager has to try to build a rapport and mutual respect. The maverick may struggle to gain support from the team and so needs the manager's backing and enthusiasm to get their ideas accepted in a group situation.

Conflict –
relational approach

Conflict is inevitable in organizations – not only because of different personalities, but also because managers are competing for resources. A bit of healthy competition is good, but it can be damaging when emotions become involved. One common theory of conflict resolution is the Interest-Based Relational (IBR) approach, based on separating the problem from personal feelings. These are the rules of this approach:

- Make sure that good relationships are the first priority: treat the other calmly and build mutual respect
- Keep people and problems separate: this allows real issues to be debated without damaging working relationships
- Pay attention to the interests that are being presented: understand why someone is adopting a particular position
- Listen first; talk second: understand where the other person is coming from before defending your own position
- Set out the facts: establish objective elements that will impact the decision
- Explore options together: a third position may exist.

Conflict resolution styles

Developed in the 1970s, the Thomas-Kilmann conflict model (TKI) helps managers understand different styles of dealing with conflict. It allows managers to understand their instinctive approach and adapt if necessary. The five styles are:

- Competitive: a firm stand, usually from a position of power; used when a decision has to be swift, but risks resentment
- Collaborative: assertive but aiming to meet needs of all parties; used when varied viewpoints will give best solution
- Compromising: tries to find a solution that will partially satisfy everyone, although everyone has to give up something; used with opponents at loggerheads or a deadline looms
- Accommodating: highly cooperative and willing to meet the needs of others at the expense of self; used when issue matters more to other parties or peace is paramount
- Avoiding: seeks to evade conflict, avoid decision-making and not hurt people's feelings; may be appropriate if victory is impossible but generally an ineffective approach.

Formal and informal teams

No matter what its structure, every organization has teams. These can be formal where the purpose is to help achieve organizational goals, or informal, where people come together and interact on a regular basis within the formal structure – for example, a group of employees running a fund-raising initiative.

Firms might use different terms to describe employees, such as associate, partner (Starbucks), microsofty (Microsoft) or tweep (Twitter), but the predominant formal team still involves people reporting to a manager. Some people may belong to more than one team, such as a senior manager who heads her own functional team, is a member of a long-standing steering committee and a member of a short-lived task force. Each team is likely to have different goals, working principles and pace of working. She may also be a member of the firm's top management team. She has to be flexible to move across different teams, building relationships with different stakeholders, and building trust when working at different levels.

Team development

American academic Dr Bruce Tuckman's four-stage theory of team development, published in 1965, has informed much work on teams ever since. Tuckman focused on the way a team develops maturity and ability, how relationships are established and how a team leader changes style. He set out four stages – known as forming, storming, norming, performing – and later added a fifth stage, adjourning and transforming:

- Forming – individuals behave independently, relying on leader for guidance and direction. Responsibilities and roles and are unclear. Team collects information, plans and bonds.
- Storming – individuals vie for position and compete with ideas; leader must facilitate and coach. Focus on goals is vital to ensure relationship issues are not a distraction.
- Norming – team agrees on values and processes, roles are clear, decisions are made together. Leader takes a step back as individuals accept responsibility.
- Performing – team has a shared vision, high autonomy and works toward a clear goal. Leader delegates and oversees.

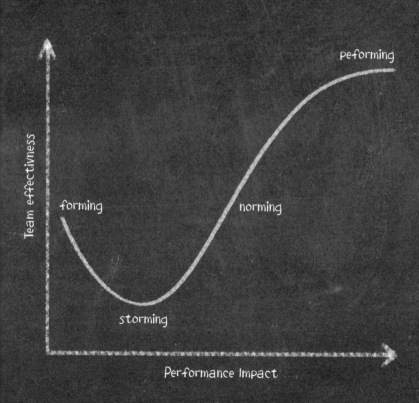

High-performance teams

High-performance teams are energetic and passionate and, because they are highly focused on their goals, are likely to achieve superior business results. Suppose a manager has a discrete project with a clear but challenging goal. She has to start by picking diverse people with complementary skills, and then typically use a democratic leadership style (see page 210) to engage team members. Allowing the team to select its own operating principles ensures a shared set of rules to govern behaviour. The manager works to create a transparent, positive, future-focused culture that will enable the team's success. Clarity with defined roles and responsibilities has to come from the manager herself. However, decisions have to be taken together and team members have to have equal access to information with open communication. Mutual trust – in each other and the team as a whole – also has to be driven from the top. Effort is focused on delivering efficiently and effectively so team members do not waste time or effort on destructive relationships; strong bonds enable high morale.

Team objectives

Knowing that each member of the team is focused on the same goal is essential for effective team performance. It provides a sense of identity, a common purpose and cohesion should obstacles arise. The manager of the team is responsible for making sure the team has clear objectives but it does not mean the manager has to dictate these. This is where a democratic style of leadership is involved.

Many managers seek to create an environment where the team can set its own objectives. Although logic might suggest teams would choose an easy option, that is rarely the case: most people will go for meaningful and achievable results that provide some stretch. The more team members are involved in agreeing what they want to achieve, the more committed they are likely to be. Team members should understand the context and overall organizational goals, and then engage in open discussion with their manager to agree what is feasible, given the available resources. The objectives should be SMART (see page 76).

Virtual teams

Virtual teams take many shapes. A manager may have team members working from home; in different cultures, geographies and time zones; or even in different organizations.

With a common goal, a clear plan and shared principles, virtual teams can be highly effective. The foundation is the manager's strong one-to-one relationship with each team member. Lack of face-to-face communication can be an issue: because team members are not seeing each other daily, relationships and trust can be hard to establish, so getting to know each other at the start can bear dividends later. Some teams share short biographies and photographs to help understand personalities and build cohesion. Team members will be reliant on technology, so investment in effective tools is a priority. Virtual meetings require even more focus on effective meeting management with a clear agenda and involvement of all participants. Managers should ensure not only that roles and responsibilities are clear, but also that activities and achievements are shared.

Team meetings

Regular, planned team meetings are the best way for individuals to come together. A manager has to work at making these meetings valuable, energizing and productive. A good idea is to get everyone to agree the purpose, the ground rules and the frequency at the outset. Timing is important, too. For example, if the CEO puts out a weekly briefing on a Wednesday, it would make sense to hold the team meeting on a Thursday so there is context with a flow of information. The 80:20 rule (see page 320) applies here. A manager should use just 20 per cent of the meeting time on top-down/organizational matters, and the remaining 80 per cent on local/ team issues.

Effective managers prepare well and share information ahead of the meeting in a consistent format, say, an update by email with any presentations as attachments. This is particularly important where people on different sites are attending the meeting by phone or video. Time together can then be used for questions, interaction and developing solutions.

Workshops

Workshops are held as needed, and are more intense than regular meetings. Typically they are held away from the workplace, require more time (at least half a day) and focus on exploring a particular subject or resolving an issue. A well planned workshop can lead to effective new ideas, strong collaborative relationships and successful problem-solving.

A workshop has to start with a purpose: the attendees should only be those who can contribute to achieving the best outcome. External speakers may help provide input. The agenda will be more complex than for a meeting: typically there will be plenary sessions, where everyone is in the same room building a shared understanding, plus breakout sessions, where smaller groups tackle a specific issue. Breakouts generally require direction on process, allocated time and expected output. The manager responsible for running a workshop needs to pay attention to detail; choice of location, good facilitation and prompt follow-up will affect the event's perceived and actual success.

Delegation

Delegation enables a manager to take on more responsibility and to develop other individuals. Coaching is inextricably linked with delegation. Together they ensure that a manager achieves a key priority: getting other people to do things.

Effective managers work out what can be delegated, and do not worry about letting go. In practice everything can be delegated, not just routine tasks. Challenging projects are a good way to develop people. Picking the most able person for a task is not always the answer: many managers pick an individual who is not yet ready to take on the task. This ensures the assignment is stretching, and so a learning opportunity. The manager has to set the person up for success with clear objectives and the necessary resources. The chosen individual or team has to understand the expected outcome and the rationale. Typically goals will be set; how the individual or team chooses to achieve those goals should be down to them. Regular support through discussion and reviews ensures the task stays on track.

Empowerment

Empowered employees have clear boundaries but also space within those boundaries to have authority and make their own decisions. Rather than allocating someone a task and expecting them to check in regularly for guidance, a manager has to allow individuals to feel responsible. Organizations that empower employees see benefits such as increased loyalty, enhanced employee skills and faster decision-making.

To foster empowerment, the organizational culture must permit risk-taking and accept mistakes from which people can learn. Managers themselves have to be prepared to let go, and team members have to *want* to be empowered; some people do not want responsibility and prefer clear direction. The manager has to be clear about roles, performance criteria and rewards. Employees also need information; they have to know about the organization's performance, competitor activity and even potentially sensitive information. They also need to understand the company's vision and values as a framework for decisions.

Coaching

Coaching is different to training. Training instructs an individual how to do something – it provides the answer. Coaching allows them to discover how they can achieve the best possible outcome – it helps the individual to find the answer. If a team member comes to ask for advice, the manager has to avoid giving an immediate answer. Rather he coaches by asking questions and listening (see page 258). Numerous coaching models, such as the GROW model developed in the 1980s, allow the manager to take an individual through a step-by-step process, and helps avoid him making his own suggestions:

- Goal: manager helps the individual create SMART goals
- Reality: manager helps the individual assess the current situation, any assumptions and what might prevent the goal from being reached
- Options: manager helps the individual consider different routes to reach the goal
- Way forward: manager helps the individual consider what they will do next and any required follow-up.

Motivation

Hope and fun. Aside from the theory (see page 308), this is a simple and memorable summary for a manager that can be applied to motivation. Hope comes not just from the work people do but from their own prospects. People want to know that they are making a difference and that their work matters to the overall organization. They want to know that, because they do their job well today, they will have opportunities to advance and better themselves. And perhaps, above all, they want a stable future. Fun is not just the occasional office party; it is about satisfaction in the job and having worthwhile relationships with colleagues. While work is serious, people want to enjoy it. Happiness is a great motivator and builds self-esteem.

Most importantly, people like to be valued. Managers can motivate people on a daily basis. Listening, making time for people and showing appreciation for a job well done with a simple 'thank you' go a long way to building a motivated team.

Entrepreneurial spirit

Many successful organizations encourage entrepreneurial spirit. It is a good way to motivate people – employees who act as if they own the business are more likely to generate ideas, challenge the status quo and feel a sense of achievement.

Managers working in such a culture need to be hands off, giving employees space to be entrepreneurial. For example, 3M allows people to use 15 per cent of their paid time to explore and come up with their own ideas, which has generated innovations such as the Post-it® Note. Managers also need to provide effective coaching. Flexible working should be encouraged as it fosters productivity and engagement. Managers must lead by example, particularly in their response to suggestions: they should never dismiss a proposal, but explore the possibilities. Mistakes should be used as learning opportunities. Strong communication across the team, building connections and collaborating with others in the organization are important. Recognition and reward also need to be aligned to entrepreneurship.

Learning from mistakes

As former US president Theodore Roosevelt said: 'The only man who never makes a mistake is the man who never does anything.' Most learning is experiential. Managers have to learn from their own mistakes and give people in their team the freedom to make mistakes from which they can learn, too. This requires a manager to let go but also create a safety net.

A manager must start with an understanding of his organization's culture and whether it encourages risk-taking, and explain this to his team. He should determine areas where a mistake would cause least damage; typically this will not be work that affects customers. This allows him to be clear about the relatively safe space where mistakes can be made. He has to encourage each employee to be open and honest about a mistake, recognize why it happened and have safeguards in place to ensure the employee will not repeat the same mistake but can learn from the experience. He should encourage them to be accountable and do what is right to fix the problem.

Self-management

A person who wants to manage others must first be able to manage himself. There are numerous aspects to this including: mental and physical health; cognitive, technical and interpersonal skills; and self-awareness. A person who tries to be a good manager but is a poor self-manager will eventually come unstuck.

A good manager is honest with himself and makes a personal assessment of his capabilities, personal organization and time management. He recognizes what he needs to change. This may seem to go against the idea of a manager being a selfless person, but it is rather like the safety advice on a plane where an adult is told to put on their oxygen mask before that of their child. Just as the adult needs the oxygen in order to help the child, so the manager has to be able to manage himself in order to manage others well. If the manager puts himself at the centre his world, he understands the importance of self-management and the impact he can have on others.

WIDER WORLD Managing contribution to society

COMMUNITY Managing friendship group

ORGANIZATION Managing upwards

DEPARTMENT/TEAM Managing work and people

FAMILY/HOME Managing personal environment

ME
Self-management

Personal impact

Actors receive feedback to help them develop presence on stage; experts guide them so they can make the right impact. And yet in business people are often reluctant to listen to feedback, which is generally about their impact on others. Personal impact involves many different factors, including personal presentation, communication and connection with others. The words used are important but communication is far more than this; it encompasses speech intonation, body language and facial expressions (see page 260). Some political and business leaders just seem to create the right impact; they are often said to have charisma. But according to a 2005 study, 50 per cent of charisma is innate and 50 per cent is learned behaviour. A manager can use this knowledge to be more self-aware and understand her own personal impact. Considering what people see and hear, and how they may feel, can be helpful. She should recognize her own strengths and weaknesses and use every opportunity for training in communication and presentation skills.

Receiving feedback

It is one thing for a manager to give feedback, but when the situation is reversed it is a natural reaction to be defensive. Feedback from a colleague or superior should not be seen as a personal attack – it is usually given because the person wants to point out a way for the manager to improve. When feedback is constructive, consistent and given by someone in an informed position, it can be beneficial. A good manager, focused on his own development, listens and then carefully considers what he has heard. He knows that the feedback is about his actions, and not about him as a person.

It is sometimes hard for an individual to recognize and understand the impact of actions or behaviours on others. It can be tempting to rush to construct an instant defence, but counting to ten at this point allows thinking time. Responding in a constructive way is a better approach and allows the manager to build on the feedback, improve or even find a new direction.

Feedback

Johari window

'O would some power the gift to give us to see ourselves as others see us,' said Scottish poet Robert Burns. It is hard for any of us to be objective about own own personalities, but a manager can at least be aware of what part she chooses to reveal in the workplace. The Johari window (so named from the first names of its inventors Joseph Luft and Harry Ingham) is a model for improving self-awareness and human interaction. A four-paned window divides awareness as follows:

1. Open self: what we are aware of and is also known to others
2. Blind spot: what we do not know about ourselves but others can see clearly
3. Hidden self: what we know about ourselves but choose not to reveal to others
4. Unknown self: aspects of ourselves that are hidden from ourselves as well as others

Each of the four areas can be changed. For example, by asking for and receiving feedback, the open self window can be expanded, so reducing the blind spot window.

	Known to me	Unknown to me
Known to others	❶ Open self	❷ Blind spot
Unknown to others	❸ Hidden self	❹ Unknown self

Influencing

The sun and wind were arguing over who was the stronger. A contest, based on who could persuade a man to remove his coat, would be the decider. The wind blew as hard as possible and the man pulled his coat closer. The sun shone and the man removed his coat. Aesop's fable is often used to illustrate influencing: people cannot be made to do something – they have to choose to do it themselves.

Well-thought-out encouragement is generally better than coercion. The latter may work occasionally, but typically has a negative impact because people resent being forced to take action. Influencing involves bringing others round to a way of thinking, almost without them realizing it. A good manager puts himself in the other person's shoes. He imagines their point of view, and develops a subtle strategy. This may mean moving slowly as he knows he cannot force the issue. He can only try to change the other person's mind through careful choice of language and behaviour and work carefully towards agreement.

Aesop's fable shows gentle persuasion (the sun) is better than force (the wind) in getting the man to take an action i.e. remove his coat.

Seven habits of highly effective people

Personal effectiveness is summarized well by Stephen Covey in his best-selling book *The 7 Habits of Highly Effective People*. These habits move people through three stages of dependence, independence and interdependence.

Habit 1 – Be proactive: highly effective people change themselves rather than reacting to external forces

Habit 2 – Begin with the end in mind: highly effective people have long-term goals based on personal principles

Habit 3 – Put first things first: make time for the things that matter in line with habit 2

Habit 4 – Think win-win: cooperate with others; avoid confrontation or win-lose approach

Habit 5 – Seek first to understand and then to be understood: the most important aspect of positive personal relationships

Habit 6 – Synergize: see potential in other people's contribution based upon the whole being greater than the sum of the parts

Habit 7 – Sharpen the saw: keep in mind the need for personal renewal: spiritual, mental, physical and social/emotional

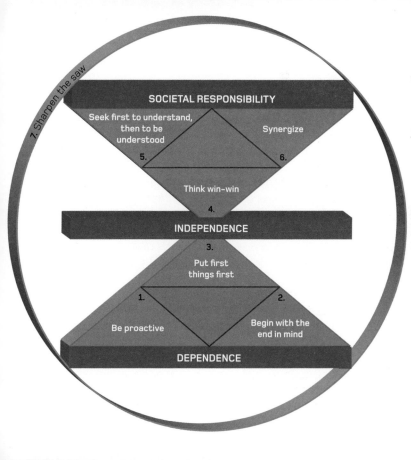

Effectiveness vs efficiency

Efficiency is doing things right, effectiveness is doing the right things: the two concepts are often confused. Suppose two people work in the same department. One may be highly efficient in terms of following the process step-by-step, keeping records and responding to emails. He appears to be good at his job. The other is less well organized, but suggests improvements and ways to do things differently. She has ideas that cut out steps in the process and so improves the quality of work from the department. This individual is more effective in her job.

Efficiency requires discipline, rigour and repetition. This may be appropriate for some standardized processes involving prescribed tasks, but it can lead to inflexibility, can discourage innovation and tends to be about the short term. Effectiveness demands that people think about how they can meet a desired goal in better ways, so encourages innovation. It is more about adapting to a changing environment as it focuses on long-term goals. Good managers should aim to be effective and efficient.

Efficient

Effective

Under-promise, over-deliver

Under-promise, over-deliver is a principle often used by effective managers. The manager who promises great things will frequently find that he then lets people down – and not always because of his own efforts. There may be factors outside his control.

On the other hand, a manager who sets realistic expectations will always satisfy others. Suppose this manager is asked to deliver a report and her boss asks how long this will take. It would be better for her to say that it will take a week and then deliver it within days. Her boss will be pleased. Whereas if she says it can be done in two days and it then takes a week her boss will be chasing her and will be disappointed. The danger in this approach is that she might get a reputation for being unambitious or lacking drive. A manager needs to take a measured view and know when it is important to agree to meet a tight deadline. Consistently exceeding others' expectations will pay dividends in the long run.

Understanding personalities

Strengths and weaknesses derive from a mix of genes and experience: understanding people's personalities can help a manager deal with others. Numerous different tests are used by organizations to assess personality, particularly during selection, because how people work together affects team performance and the organization's success. One of the most commonly used personality tests is the Myers-Briggs Type Indicator (MBTI), developed in the 1940s, based on psychological types described by psychiatrist Carl Jung. By measuring four preferences (shown opposite), it categorizes people into 16 different personality types: the essence of MBTI is that seemingly random variation in behaviour is actually orderly and consistent, due to the way people tend to use perception and judgement. Perception is the way a person becomes aware of things and judgement is how a person reaches conclusions on what they have perceived. If people differ in these two fundamental ways then it is likely that they will differ not just in their interests and values but also in their skills and motivation.

Extraversion (E)
focuses perception and judgement on people and objects
Introversion (I)
focuses perception and judgement on concepts and ideas

Sensing (S)
pays attention to facts or happenings through one or more of
the five senses
Intuition (N)
thinks through meanings, relationships and possibilities, and often
reads between the lines

Thinking (T)
makes decisions impersonally on basis of logical consequences
Feeling (F)
relies primarily on the basis of personal or social values

Judgement (J)
favours judgement process (thinking or feeling)
Perception(P)
favours a perceptive process (sensing or intuition)

Dealing with distractions

Distractions are a fact in today's workplace, but they affect output and motivation: not getting through the day's work can lead to frustration and stress. How can a manager handle such daily disturbances – from office gossip to constant emails?

Blocking distractions is about focus, managing time and finding the right space to work. Good managers start by using technology in a way that does not involve constant interruptions. Some switch off their mobile phones when they need to concentrate, others deal with emails only at a certain time of day. Time management involves prioritizing; some managers may block out their diaries, or let their team know they are focused on a particular piece of work and don't want to be interrupted. Open-plan offices increase distractions: it can be hard to ignore constant phone calls, conversations and others walking by to ask questions. Finding a quiet corner, booking a meeting room or working from home can enable concentration to achieve what needs to be done.

Elephants

The elephant in the room is an issue that everyone can see because it is so big, but no one wants to talk about or deal with. An example might be when a whole meeting is spent in totally superficial discussion because no one wants to mention the real subject. Elephants are best dealt with, rather than letting them run wild. If an issue is left unresolved because of seemingly good intentions, such as wanting to avoid conflict, it wastes time, damages trust and causes missed opportunities.

Effective managers take control of elephants before they become destructive. Voicing the issue is a good first step – often there is a huge sigh of relief. Then the problem can be addressed. Frequently it is about unrealistic expectations; people know a deadline cannot be met. Open and honest conversation allows misperceptions to be addressed. People may find it uncomfortable but, with careful guidance, an effective manager will ensure a powerful process that helps strengthen relationships and allows progress to be made.

Personal development

Personal development occurs as we learn from experiences. Some people do this more naturally than others: they continually seek out opportunities to grow and learn. Others may need to create a personal development plan and take a more structured approach. Some organizations even have management development teams to support their managers.

People who become managers are more likely to be self-aware and know what they want from life. A good manager uses this to know his strengths and weaknesses, potential and ambitions, and creates a plan to acquire new skills, knowledge or methods of working. The aim is do his current job better and to progress. He sets himself achievable goals, identifies actions required and what support or intervention is required to achieve them. Thinking of development as spanning a range of opportunities is a trait of successful managers. This could include, for example, reading business books, learning a new language or attending a course on a specific skill such as project management.

Work-life balance

The boundaries between work and personal life are steadily being eroded. Technology makes us accessible 24/7 – it was supposed to free up time, but people now spend more time than ever glued to screens. This can be damaging for health and for relationships with family and friends. Finding the right balance requires the individual to be disciplined and take action.

Self-help author Stephen Covey (see page 170) suggests that people should manage their time by recognizing and prioritizing the importance of relationships – as well as work, people have different roles and needs such as family, work, community, personal time and recreation. Covey's time management model is based on the principle that a person should manage time around what is important, not what is urgent – and that this approach should be carried through and planned across a person's different roles. If people concentrate on highly important, but non-urgent issues, across all their identified roles they can balance work and other priorities successfully.

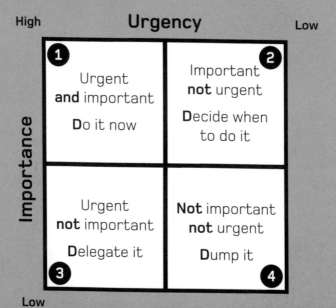

Time management

'There are never enough hours in the day.' Yet everyone has the same 24 hours. The issue is not time itself, but a manager's workload and how he uses his time effectively to get through it. Managing time defines a person's productivity, personality and performance.

Effective managers think of time as a valuable resource. They recognize that they cannot do everything, and prioritize and plan every day to control their use of time. Starting with goals and focusing on objectives rather than activities can help eliminate time-wasting tasks. A daily to-do list that has priorities and time estimates, rather than random actions, will ensure the important things get done. The list should build in time for unexpected events. Some people are simply busy being busy, but effective time management is about quality not quantity. Successful managers get on with things rather than procrastinating, do things right first time and finish what they start, rather than leaping from one unfinished task to the next.

The power of three

'Don't try to do everything. Pick three things and do them well.' It is good advice: the manager gains recognition for the three things done well, and other things may even be forgotten if they are not important. Time management advice relies on prioritization, and by picking three things a manager can focus on achieving success rather than worrying about all the things they don't have time to do. Some managers may think three is not enough, but the key is to group things accordingly. For example, a manager might aim for three goals and pick three objectives to help reach each of them. Choosing threes is a way of keeping things simple, memorable and achievable.

There is something about the number three: it has legendary power across many cultures and is referenced frequently in nature, religion and science. The concept of using three for emphasis is used in writing, presentations and law, as in, for example, 'the truth, the whole truth, and nothing but the truth'. And threes can work well in many different situations.

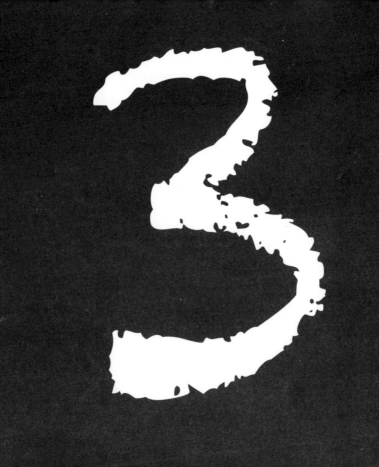

Coping mechanisms

Today's workplace can be stressful. Internalizing an issue can lead to self-blame; wherever possible it is best to talk things through with colleagues. In some cases a manager has to adjust his expectations or recognize what he cannot change. Developing personal coping mechanisms can help deal with stressful situations. Some positive approaches include:

- Taking a walk during the lunch break: fresh air and time away from the computer screen helps restore balance
- Physical activity: regular exercise, such as running or team sports, is a good way to handle stress
- Relaxation: calming techniques, or activities such as yoga, can help manage stress and improve overall coping
- Music: listening to calming music to and from work can help with positive thoughts
- Humour: seeing the funny side of things can help deal with awkward situations or mistakes
- Support: family and friends can provide a friendly ear and support during stressful times.

Managing upwards

As well as managing a team, every manager has to think about managing his own manager: the boss. Why? A manager needs his boss to provide resources, take actions, to help with his next career move – and to ensure he still has a job.

A manager has to get to know his boss, understand how she likes to receive information and what she values as important – and then adapt his style to suit. He should only ever present facts, avoid personal views and be clear about what he expects his boss to do. No boss likes surprises; she would rather be forewarned and forearmed. If a manager makes a mistake, he should tell his boss before someone else does. The boss does not want problems that a manager should be able to resolve himself, but wants to get involved where she can bring influence or add something to the solution. A manager should always deliver on commitments to his boss, helping to build credibility. Most importantly, a manager should always make his boss look good.

Networking

'It's not what you know, it's who you know' – an old adage that still holds true. A manager needs to work at building a network of colleagues to help develop in her present role and to open up future opportunities. Networking within an organization begins with being genuinely interested in everyone as a foundation for building strong relationships.

External networking requires more planning and effort – the manager has to decide who she wants to meet – from functional peers to a wider range of people in her sector. Face-to-face opportunities may involve conferences, breakfast meetings and business clubs – joining a regular group is more likely to result in enduring relationships. Never assume anything at a first meeting – being interested and asking open questions can reveal unlikely connections. Networking via social media is also increasingly important. An up-to-date profile is vital, and relevant groups on sites such as LinkedIn can lead to contacts that might previously have taken a lengthy series of introductions.

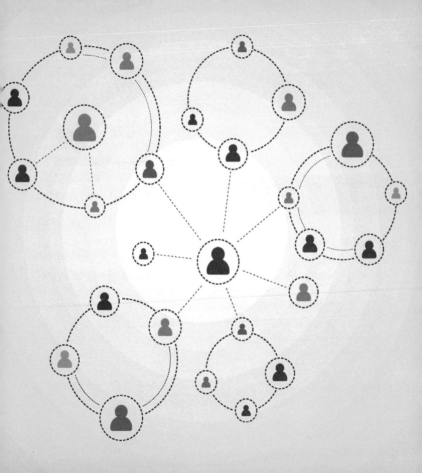

Career management

'If you don't know where you are going, you might wind up someplace else,' warned American baseball coach Yogi Berra. Successful managers have a clear view of where they want to be in a number of years' time, and a plan for how they will get there. This may involve taking a number of carefully planned steps and career moves.

Suppose a technical specialist in a food manufacturing business has progressed to become manager of the firm's food research team but knows there are few possible promotions from there. He wants to be a general manager in the business but has neither the skills nor experience. The best way for him to progress might be to take a sideways move to become a production manager in the manufacturing plant because this opens up other opportunities. Many firms have explicit processes to support career progression. This is a win-win as it helps individuals build and develop their careers, and enables the organization to grow and retain valuable talent.

Cobbler's children

'The cobbler's children have no shoes.' This old expression, referring to the fact that the cobbler is too busy making other people's shoes to make them for his own family, is often used to describe the quirk whereby tradesmen or professionals are so busy working for clients that they neglect to use their skills in their personal lives. Oft-quoted examples are the decorator who is too busy painting other people's houses to keep his own in order, and the accountant who is too busy working for other people to submit his own tax return.

Human resources is often used as an example in business, where HR professionals understand the need for career management yet often fail to have plans in place for themselves. No manager wants to gain such a reputation – each must ensure that professional and personal issues are addressed and managed in the same efficient and effective way. Equal attention to professional and personal finances is just one example.

Professional behaviour

Professionalism is a mix of what a person does in his particular role, his behaviour and his personal presentation. In the workplace it is more likely that someone would comment on something being unprofessional rather than make a positive comment. And yet professional behaviour is vital for a manager to succeed. Much of it is downright good manners or common sense, such as showing respect for others, being honest and delivering quality work.

Most organizations have written codes of behaviour, but there are also unwritten professional standards in every organization that a manager must be aware of. Some fall into the category of basic courtesies and range from being punctual for meetings to not using seniority to queue jump at the coffee machine. Others may require careful observation. For example, everyone might wear jeans on dress-down Friday but only with leather shoes and not with trainers. The important thing for a manager is to find out the unspoken rules and stick by them so he fits in.

Management styles

It would seem reasonable to think that different people would each have their own distinctive style of management. However, research carried out by consulting firm Hay McBer, and drawing on a random sample of nearly 4,000 managers worldwide, shows that, in fact, there are just six main management styles. Managers should understand this, and be sufficiently self-aware not to get stuck with just one style. To be successful, a manager should aim to adapt and use many different styles, according to the situation and people involved.

In an article for the *Harvard Business Review*, author Daniel Goleman likened these different leadership styles to golf clubs in a seasoned professional player's bag: just as the golfer has to choose the correct club for each shot so a manager has to choose the correct style for each situation. The six styles, explained in more detail on the following pages, are: Coercive, Authoritative, Affiliative, Democratic, Pacesetting and Coaching.

Coercive style

The coercive style of management is perhaps most simply defined as the 'do what I tell you' approach. The manager issues orders and expect others to follow. This top-down style demands compliance and is essentially about management by fear. People do as they are told, and there is no discussion. The manager is clearly in charge and does not invite others' opinions. Typically, this is the least effective style, with results that can be damaging to the organization; people do not feel valued or respected. Motivation is low because people feel no sense of responsibility, and as they have no sense of ownership for their tasks, they do not feel accountable. They have little satisfaction in their work and may lose sight of the overall direction of the organization. Innovation can be stifled. As such, this style should only be used in a crisis, for example: to kick-start a turnaround, in a hostile takeover situation, or with difficult employees when other styles have failed. It requires caution and should only be used as a short-term measure, since the effect on morale can be damaging.

Authoritative style

Best summed up as the 'come with me' approach, the authoritative management style is used by managers with the ability to articulate a long-term vision and encourage people to commit and work to achieve that vision. People are enthusiastic and understand how their area of work fits with the bigger picture, but are given the freedom to make their own decisions to achieve that vision. The manager creates clarity so that people are focused on a common purpose, and this can be highly motivating. This style can have a positive impact because people are empowered and have a certain amount of flexibility. They have the freedom to innovate and take calculated risks, knowing that progress towards the vision is the standard by which they will be measured.

This style can be used in almost any business situation, but especially when a business needs new direction and fresh long-term vision. It may be less effective when a manager is working with people who have more expertise in a particular area.

Affiliative style

The affiliative or 'people come first' approach works when a manager is good at building positive relationships through creating personal and emotional bonds. He strives to be liked by his team, and so communicates openly and shares ideas. The group tends to be harmonious, morale is high and there is strong loyalty to the manager. The working style is flexible as the manager is hands-off, encouraging innovation and risk taking. The manager always tries to focus on positive feedback, often allowing individuals leeway and to find their own way to improvement. He is likely to take his individual direct reports out for a meal or a drink after work, and to celebrate team achievements.

This style is best used when a team needs harmony, when morale needs improving or where trust has been an issue. However, it may not be suitable where there are issues of poor performance. It can be combined with the authoritative style to ensure the team has a clear sense of direction.

Democratic style

The 'what do you think?' approach to management involves a manager seeking consensus within her team. She spends time getting people's views and 'buy-in' to team objectives, and drives their commitment by allowing them to have a say in decisions, individual goals and the way that work is carried out. People are involved in discussions on strategy and tactics, and on the way progress is assessed. Morale in this kind of environment is high because open communication allows people to voice their concerns, all of which builds trust and respect. A major drawback of this style, however, can be endless meetings because consensus is hard to achieve. What's more, some managers who use this style do so to avoid making decisions, and this can lead to confusion and even conflict.

This style is best used when the manager is unsure of the best path to take and has a group of highly talented employees with access to as much information as she has herself. It is not appropriate when a crisis requires rapid decisions and action.

Pacesetting style

The 'do as I do, now' approach known as the pacesetting style involves the manager setting high-performance standards for which he is the exemplar. He may be obsessive about doing things faster and better, and expects others to do the same. Poor performers are singled out, and it is made clear that more is expected from them – if they cannot raise their game, they are replaced by people who can achieve more. In principle, this style might be expected to drive performance and deliver results, but this is not always the case: employees can feel overwhelmed by the manager's constant expectations, and research shows that morale can often drop. A manager may be so focused on being quicker and smarter that he fails to bring people with him. In urging people to keep up the pace, he fails to give feedback, and followers may feel that they are hurtling in an unknown direction. As a result, this style is only productive when leading highly self-motivated, competent staff with strong technical skills. Here, it is likely that the team's ability and work style will match the manager's expectations.

Coaching style

The coaching or 'try this' approach sees the manager focus on people development, rather than on immediate tasks. She helps individuals identify strengths and weaknesses and establish their own goals, and works with them to build a plan so they can achieve their career aspirations. Such managers delegate: employees are given challenging assignments that stretch them, even if this means that the task may not be completed on time. The manager gives regular feedback and is in constant communication with direct reports. Morale and commitment are all high. The working environment is positive and people are prepared to be flexible and take risks knowing that they have their manager's support.

This style requires significant time commitment from the manager, but can be used in any business situation. It is a powerful tool, particularly in an environment where learning and experimentation are encouraged and employees have strong self-awareness and a desire to better themselves.

Situational leadership

Situational Leadership was developed by Paul Hersey in *The Situational Leader*, and Ken Blanchard in *The One Minute Manager*. It requires managers to change their leadership style based on the maturity of the people involved and the details of the task. Using this approach, they can place the right level of emphasis on the task, or on people relationships, depending on what is needed to get the job done successfully. Four leadership styles are split between task-oriented and people-oriented:

Task-oriented
Telling: manager tells his people what to do and how to do it
Selling: manager provides information and direction, but with more communication to get people on board

People-oriented
Participating: manager focuses more on relationship and less on direction; he works with his team and shares decision-making
Delegating: manager passes most of the responsibility to his team; he monitors progress, but is less involved in decisions.

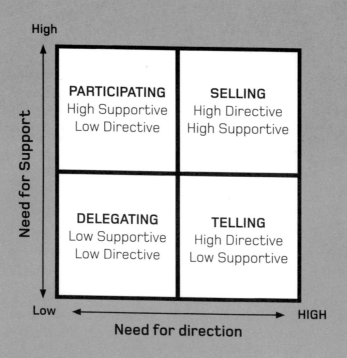

Authentic leadership

Authentic leadership is based on the concept that a leader's style has to be consistent with their personality and core values, and that this is honest, ethical and practical. The concept was introduced by Bill George in his book *Authentic Leadership*. Such leaders display consistent qualities: understanding their purpose, practising their values, leading with their heart and demonstrating self-discipline. They are concerned less with money and power, more with empowering people, and are led by their beliefs. They are dedicated to personal growth, and committed to building strong relationships and sustainable organizations. Events and experiences in their own lives provide inspiration; they face up to mistakes and so find ways to overcome shortcomings, making them stronger.

George argues that anyone can become an authentic leader through hard work and developing their leadership qualities. But having developed their leadership style, this should not be overly rigid, and should be adaptable to different situations.

Management by walking around

It is hard to imagine that management by walking around (MBWA) was so well received in the 1980s; it seems obvious. But at a time when managers were typically behind desks and even behind closed doors, the concept encouraged face-to-face communication. And today, in a time when technology, particularly email, has made much of modern communication impersonal, MBWA is once more in vogue.

MBWA is an effective way for a manager to connect with people. Getting out and encouraging informal discussion can help build relationships. MBWA does not have to be taken literally: it is simply about recognizing the importance of informal chat to building relationships. The trick is for a manager to be relaxed; to ask questions, to listen and observe rather than talk, and to seek feedback and ideas. For example, a manager could choose to wander to another floor and sit at a team member's desk for an informal meeting, rather than call them to her desk, or she could choose to sit with a different colleague for coffee or lunch.

Solving problems

Problems can be a distraction from the day job. It can be exciting to step in and start fighting a fire, but this uses precious time and energy. Busybody managers get involved in problems where there is no need. Effective managers keep their heads down and focus on what they have to achieve, and so pick the right problems.

The 80:20 rule comes into play again (see page 320). Eighty per cent of the problems that happen from day to day are unlikely to require a manager's input. Some problems may be part of the daily routine and resolution happens as part of a colleague's responsibility. Other problems may simply be resolved by events. The remaining 20 per cent of the problems are more likely to be issues that are important and urgent and need to be addressed: if left unresolved, they may impact on productivity or objectives. Even if a manager is certain that a problem is important, he might have to be wary about getting involved because of internal politics.

To Do

☐ Sort other people's problems

☐

☐

☐

Prioritizing problems

So how does a manager pick the right problems? Three questions help determine whether a problem is a priority:

- Is the problem important? A manager has to ask if the problem impacts achievement of his overall objectives and whether, if it is not resolved, there will be significant consequences. Is there a stop-gap solution that might prevent things getting worse?
- Is the problem urgent? Will waiting make the problem worse, or make no difference? Some problems have a way of resolving themselves as more information comes to light. If people are involved, someone else might take action that changes things. If it is urgent he should act immediately. If not, see what tomorrow brings.
- Is this problem actionable? Not every problem is going to be within a manager's control. Such problems can be irritating, but it may be that he has to develop coping mechanisms and learn to live with issues he cannot directly influence or resolve.

The exam question

Most people will remember being told, before school exams, to 'read the question': a student gets no marks for displaying deep knowledge of King Henry VI and the War of the Roses if the question is about Henry VIII and his six wives. Knowing and understanding the exam question is always the starting point.

It is the same in business. A good way to start considering a problem is to ask 'What is the exam question?' This focuses the mind. Just as a student get no marks for answering the wrong question, a manager gets no credit for addressing the wrong problem. However, while the exam question is clearly stated for the student, a manager has to work out the real problem before he can start to find the answer. A junior manager's problems are more likely to be clear-cut, but seniority brings complexity and exposure to larger strategic issues. Yet the first step always has to be the same: to have a clear, written statement of the problem being addressed.

Crisis or opportunity?

Former US president John F. Kennedy once said 'The Chinese word crisis is composed of two characters, representing danger and opportunity'. Although apparently a mistranslation, Kennedy's aphorism offers a powerful way of thinking: when a problem arises it is uncomfortable. The sense of impending crisis can create a fight or flight reaction, and this can be a catalyst for action or a cause of confusion.

A manager has to acknowledge the situation, discover the cause of the problem and then involve others in finding a solution. This creates the opportunity to challenge the status quo and look at a situation through a new lens. Since problems often have knock-on effects, they might also allow a manager to look at broader issues. This creates the right environment for change and improvement, whereas previously people might have been fearful of disrupting the status quo. And it is also likely that valuable lessons will be learnt, which can take the business forward.

Asking the
right questions

Spot the difference between these questions: 'How do we solve this problem?' and 'What is the problem we are trying to solve?' It is easy to step into problem-solving mode even before the problem has been understood, but effective problem-solving and decision-making involves suspending judgement and asking the right questions. There is a saying: 'To assume makes an ass out of you and me'. Managers have to avoid assumptions and be curious for information about the problem.

The best questions are open-ended, and start with the words that Rudyard Kipling called his six honest serving-men: who, what, when, where, why and how. Asking the right questions helps to define a problem and creates a better picture of the issues. It also involves people and builds a commitment to resolution. But of course, it's equally important to listen to the answers: managers must let go of their own views and preconceptions. The resulting multiple options can be further explored and are likely to produce a better solution.

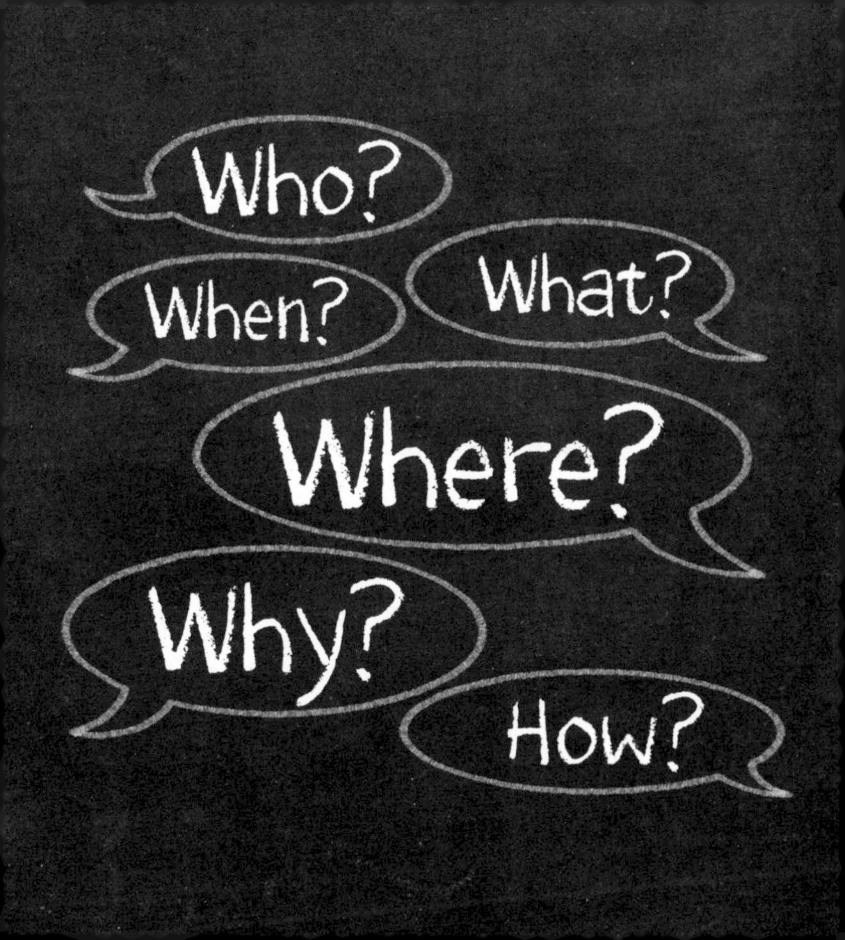
Who?
When?
What?
Where?
Why?
How?

Establishing the facts

'Houston we have a problem.' This slightly misquoted piece of understatement from the Apollo 13 astronauts has since been widely used to play down any kind of trouble. Problems are typically a deviation from that which is normal or expected – in business, they are often called 'issues', perhaps to diminish associations with blame. Problems come in all shape and sizes, from non-delivery of raw materials to security alerts. The first may slow down production and affect orders but the second potentially has life-threatening consequences.

The starting point in any situation is to establish the facts and to make an assessment. The key for any manager is to remain calm and keep a sense of perspective. Nothing can be assumed until the facts are known, and it is important to get to the source of the information as key points may be lost as the story is passed on. What's more, people tend to generalize. Sticking the key 'who, what, when, where, why and how' questions will help establish accurate facts.

NASA managers examine an improvised air filter designed to save the lives of the Apollo 13 astronauts. The starting point to solving any problem is always to establish the facts.

Cause and effect

Separating cause from effect is important. A cause is why something happens, and effect is what happens because of the cause. A manager may start exploring the problem of late delivery of goods to a customer, and discover that this is the effect of a deeper problem that needs to be probed.

A cause-and-effect diagram, often called a fishbone diagram, can be a useful tool. This concept was developed in the 1960s by Professor Kaoru Ishikawa, a pioneer in quality management. The starting point is to describe the problem at the fish's head. A manager then needs to work with his team to identify all the potential reasons why the problem has occurred. These causes should include everything from people and procedures to materials and equipment. Each cause can then be broken down further into sub-causes – for example, a people cause could have sub-causes such as slow recruitment and lack of training. Once complete, the fish diagram is analysed – in a complex business, it is likely to reveal multiple causes.

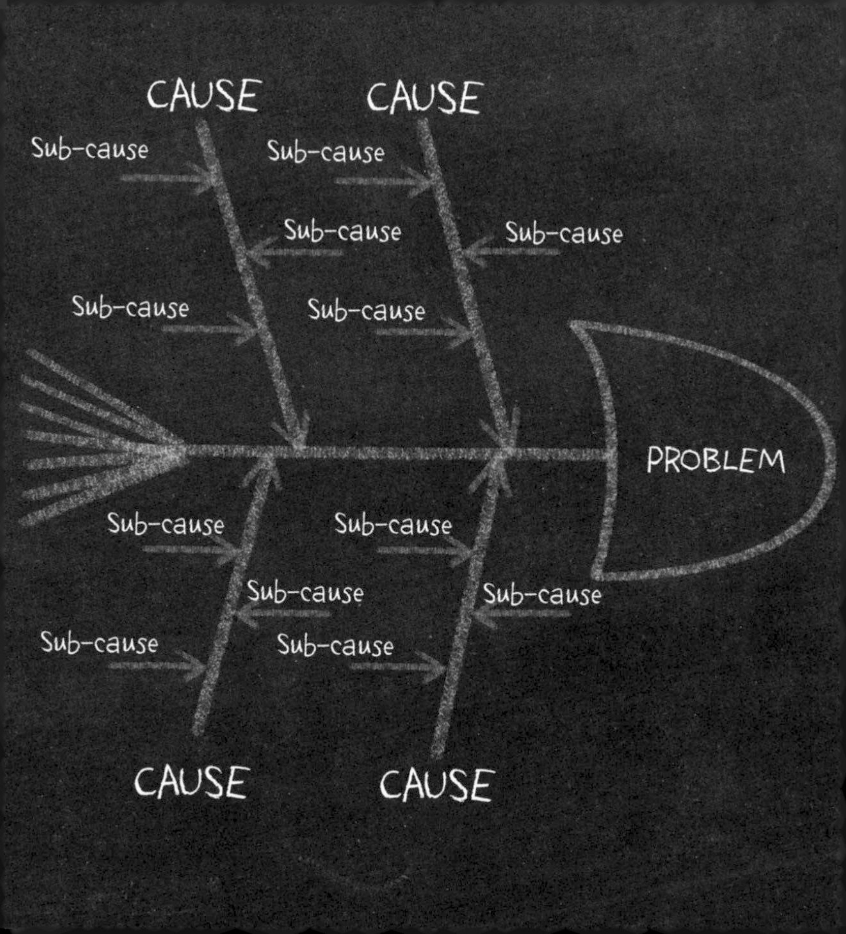
CAUSE
CAUSE
Sub-cause
Sub-cause
Sub-cause
Sub-cause
Sub-cause
Sub-cause
PROBLEM
Sub-cause
Sub-cause
Sub-cause
Sub-cause
Sub-cause
Sub-cause
CAUSE
CAUSE

Root cause analysis

Another tool that can help a manager understand why a problem has occurred, Root Cause Analysis (RCA) seeks to identify the origin of a problem using five steps to find the primary cause. RCA assumes that systems and events are interrelated: an action in one area has a knock-on effect in another. By tracing these actions backwards, a manager can discover where the trouble started and how it grew to be the problem she now faces. The key steps are:

1. Define the problem – what happened, what are the effects?
2. Collect data – how long has the problem existed and what is the impact (considering all stakeholders)?
3. Identify possible causal factors – consider physical causes, human causes and organizational causes, and create a cause-and-effect diagram (see page 234).
4. Identify the root cause – find the real reason the problem occurred; ask 'why?' until the root of the problem is revealed.
5. Recommend and implement lasting solutions.

Why? because...
Why? because...
Why? because...
Why? because...
Why? because...

Brainstorming

No manager has the answer to every problem. He will need to use the collective ideas, knowledge and experience of others in the organization to understand the problem and resolve it. In doing so, he should avoid political expediency, choosing the best solution, rather than the most popular.

One technique that can be used to consider a problem is brainstorming: working together, a varied group of people generates numerous ideas on a specific issue and then determines objectively which idea(s) provides the best solution. Participants should come from various departments across the organization, so that each brings a different perspective of the issue. Getting people together to explore a problem encourages creative thinking, helps build teams and encourages ownership of the solution. Effective facilitation, ensuring the group is allowed to voice ideas or issues before they are analysed, will help the group generate solutions that no single individual would have been likely to reach on their own.

Breakthrough thinking

Brainstorming was popular in the 1980s and 1990s, and can certainly yield results, but the ideas and solutions it generates are typically based on *known* facts. In today's business environment, managers are often asked to go beyond this – to discover what they *don't know* and find transformational solutions that unlock potential in the organization.

Breakthrough thinking is one process that aims to do just this. It starts with a manager identifying something that is known to be a major problem, but is thought to be too big or contentious to tackle, such as the volume of customer complaints. The discussion approaches the problem from an entirely different perspective – for example, by considering feedback from *satisfied* customers. A small group (no more than four) is formed from people who are immersed in the problem, so bring deep knowledge and experience. Parameters are defined, and thinking is challenged to go beyond the current problem to envision how the organization could be different when the problem is solved.

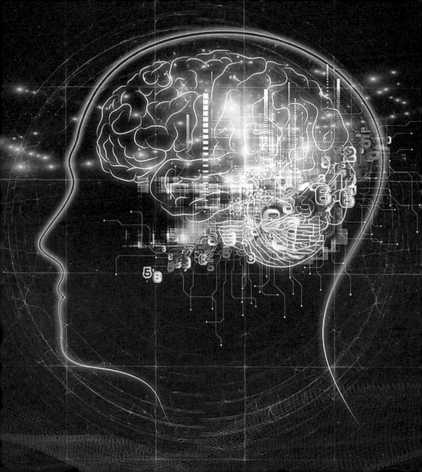

Avoiding the decision escalator

Decisions have to be taken day in day out in business. What any manager has to avoid is that he stands at the top of the escalator waiting for every decision to come up to him. People working at different levels in the organization have to know that they can make decisions on certain things and what type of issues need escalation. They also need to know what level of detail their manager will need to make a decision.

A well-designed organization, where roles and responsibilities are clear, can enable the decision-making process. Some firms set criteria for escalation, such as the value of a customer order. Organizational culture will have an influence because employees have to know that if they make a decision and it is wrong they will not be penalized. Decisions become more complex in a matrix organization because any one manager may not have all the information. Close collaboration between peers in different functions, such as operations and marketing, can help provide clarity about decision-making responsibility.

Is there a right
or wrong decision?

There is no such thing as a perfect decision – there are always going to be trade-offs. A manager is likely to be faced with conflicting priorities; achieving one objective may put another at risk. But making any decision, even the wrong one, may be better than no decision.

Suppose a manager is faced with a decision on a possible factory closure. She is likely to gather facts and carry out thorough analysis, but she will also be offered differing opinions from team members and colleagues – it is easy for her to be side-tracked. With pressure from different people, she must be objective and use her own judgement to pick what *she* believes is the best option. Sometimes the decision is obvious but unpalatable: a weak manager, or one concerned about personal popularity, may try to hedge her bets or even avoid the decision altogether. In other situations, fear of making the wrong choice may prevent a decision. Individual inertia can be damaging in business, wasting valuable time and resources.

Risk management

Managing risk is an important task for both profit and non-profit organizations. Maintaining a comprehensive risk register – with a brief descriptor, allocated responsibility and prioritization – enables a full picture of the organization's exposure to risk. Regular review and constant updating ensures the register is a living document that enables risks to be addressed and opportunities to be identified. Prioritization involves risk weighting, typically by combining a factor for probability with a factor for level of impact. Managers have to be cautious of basing likelihood of outcome on past performance, particularly in a rapidly changing world.

Determining response to a risk ensures that risk management provides real value. Managers have to consider three options: avoidance, minimization or acceptance. Risk avoidance might mean changing a supplier, risk minimization might mean improving a process, while risk acceptance might involve action such as taking out insurance.

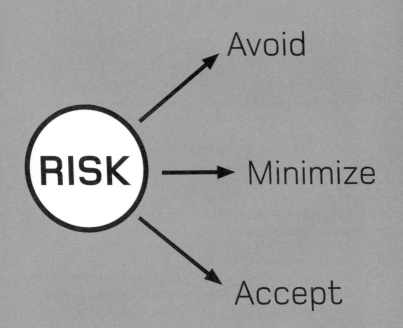

Swift decisions

A manager may sometimes be in a position where he has to make a decision based on limited information. Delaying the decision leads to uncertainty in the team and means that things cannot progress. It can also damage a manager's reputation as he will be seen as indecisive (see page 36).

Danish organization theorists Kristian Kreiner and Søren Christensen encourage managers to make decisions swiftly despite minimal information. This requires courage but allows a manager to have greater impact. Their model shows how the consequences of a manager's decision relate directly to the extent of knowledge available: the less knowledge, the greater the consequences and vice versa. A good example might be the start of a large-scale project where details are still unclear: early decisions are fundamental to get the project underway and will have far-reaching consequences. When the project is at a later stage there will be more information, but decisions to be taken will have less influence on the final outcome.

The Consequences Model

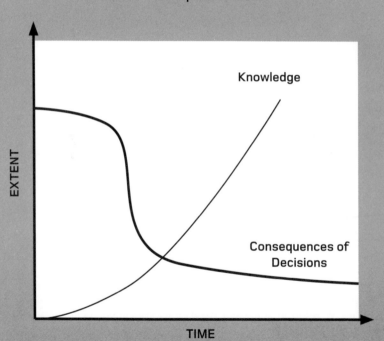

Intuition

Call it intuition, gut feeling or a hunch, but the ability to make quick decisions on limited information is a valuable instinct in any modern organization. This ability to use 'soft factors' rather than hard data is innate in some: psychologist Carl Jung believed that some people do not use concrete sensory experiences but rely on abstract intuition (see page 176). There is also a view that intuition can develop with experience in business. For example, a more experienced manager draws his intuition from similar past situations, and equally the better his intuition the more able he is to identify and swiftly assimilate relevant facts.

Organizations generally favour managers who step forward with a view, even if it is based on a hunch. It saves time, particularly if huge amounts of data are available. Detail and analysis can derail decisions – the more information, the harder the decision, and a perfect solution rarely exists anyway. What is more, a decision based on intuition is likely to be practical because it draws on understanding of previous outcomes.

The recency effect

As a psychological phenomenon, the recency effect explains why individuals are more likely to remember things that come at the end of a list, but it can also affect decision-making.

In busy organizations, where people are regularly having conversations with different people, some individuals tend to be easily swayed by the ideas of the last person they spoke to. Suppose a manager has been working with his team on a project for some time but has not yet made a key decision. He then has a casual conversation by the water cooler just before a key meeting, and a chance bit of information discussed there influences his decision. This can be frustrating for others involved in a project, as the manager has ignored all the earlier good work. This extra, and sometimes irrelevant, information can cause the project to deviate from its objectives. The recency effect can also affect performance appraisals – an individual's most recent activities are likely to be foremost in the manager's mind, rather than the entire year's efforts.

Communication

Communication is the way that messages and information flow around an organization: up, down and across. It is also the way in which messages and information flow out of the organization to customers and stakeholders (who in turn communicate with the organization and other stakeholders). Communication is continuous, hard to control and so powerful that it can make or break a company or a manager's career.

At one end of the scale, poor communication can lead to problems in a team, including misunderstandings, loss of trust and demotivation, while at the other end of the scale a choice of the wrong words in a presentation can bring a company to its knees. One of the most infamous examples of this is Gerald Ratner, chairman of the Ratner jewellery group. In a 1991 speech to the UK's Institute of Directors, he tried to make a joke by describing a product as 'total crap', but the comment came over as contempt for his customers: shares plummeted and the firm nearly collapsed.

What is good communication?

Good communication once simply had to be timely and relevant. Today, however, it encompasses all the words a manager speaks, the emails he writes, and even his authenticity. Behaviour is the most powerful mode of communication; it must match with written and spoken words in order to build trust.

Messages have to be simple; people are constantly bombarded with information and are time-poor. A manager has to be clear about context, facts and what action he expects from people, but must also be genuine. Too often managers read speeches, deliver presentations or send emails written by someone else – this comes over as corporate speak. Good managers find and use their own distinctive voice. Being seen is just as important as being heard. Face-to-face meetings enable two-way conversation and help build relationships. Active listening, asking open questions and using observation skills are important. People may be fearful of speaking out to those in authority, so being able to pick up non-verbal signals is vital.

Active listening

Being a successful manager requires a person to be a good listener. Active listening allows a manager to understand information more swiftly, to demonstrate concern and to encourage people to be more open. It is a skill that can be learnt, and which improves with practice.

A good listener establishes eye contact, without staring. She shuts out other thoughts and focuses on what the speaker is saying; this can be difficult as there will usually be many other pressures and distractions. She nods or shows she is listening with an occasional smile or affirmation. Body language is important, so she leans forward, for example, rather than sitting back with her arms folded. She is also alert to the speaker's posture and tone of voice; these help her to understand the speaker's attitude and intentions. A good listener will not interrupt, but at the end will reiterate what she believes she has been told and, if needed, will ask relevant questions to clarify understanding (see page 262).

Body language

Body language is a powerful concept that says a great deal about self-confidence and attitude. Body posture, arm movements and facial gestures all combine to give non-verbal signals and convey messages without a person realising it. Experts believe that non-verbal signals account for around 80 per cent of a message received. For example, folding arms is a sign of negativity, while fidgeting indicates nervousness.

Suppose a manager calls a meeting to tell his team that he is happy with the quarterly results, but does so with a scowl on his face, a wagging finger and leaning menacingly across the table. The impact will not be positive, and his team will take away a mixed message. When a manager is in contact with people it is impossible not to communicate. Just shaking a person's hand or looking them in the eye means something. Being aware of body language is important, and this is an area where training can often help. Successful managers smile; it has a universal positive impact.

SUMMIT ORGANIZA
EXPEDITI
NINETE

Checking understanding

In any situation, it is always worth checking that the listener has understood the message. Clarification is a vital way of avoiding misunderstandings: a manager should ask whether the listener has understood, and even ask them to summarize and playback. This is particularly important if there needs to be clear action and a manager needs to know who is going to do what and by when. Equally, if a manager has been briefed by someone else and is in any doubt, he should say: 'Can I just play back to you what I have understood?'

Communicating to diverse, international groups adds another dynamic, particularly because of non-verbal signals and the fact that gestures may have different meanings. For example, in most countries people nod their head to mean yes and shake their head to mean no, but in some parts of the world these meanings are reversed. Good managers familiarize themselves with cultural norms when presenting to a diverse audience, and always check understanding when doing international business.

Manager communication skills

Almost every job advertisement for a managerial role lists good communications skills as essential. No matter how much a person knows, if she can't get her message over in the organization, she will not be able to make things happen.

What can a manager do to ensure she excels at communication? Simplicity, consistency and repetition is the most effective mantra. By continually thinking of ways to simplify or illustrate concepts and outcomes she can sharpen her message. Preparation for every meeting ensures she knows what she wants to convey. She schedules time for individual and team communication in her diary, and makes time to explain things to people so that they understand. She knows that people will not remember a presentation so she tells them what she is *going* to tell them, she *tells* them, and then she *reminds them* what she has told them. Astute managers know that people like and remember stories far more than facts and figures, so she develops her ability to use anecdotes and build narratives.

Message, audience and channels

When a manager needs to communicate, he has to think about his message, his audience and the best channel for reaching them. These three aspects are inter-related:

- Message – Why send the message? What is the objective? Is it purely informational, or do people need to take action – and if so, when? The message needs to be clear, concise and compelling. Kipling's 'six men' may help in drafting the message (see page 230)
- Audience – Who needs to know? The audience will influence the tone and language of the message, and whether any context needs to be set. It may be that different audiences need different messages on the same topic
- Channels – different channels have different impacts and can achieve a different objective. If a manager wants to create awareness by distributing information, he may choose to send an email. Where his objective is to get commitment to an initiative, more face-to-face communication is involved, with greater time invested.

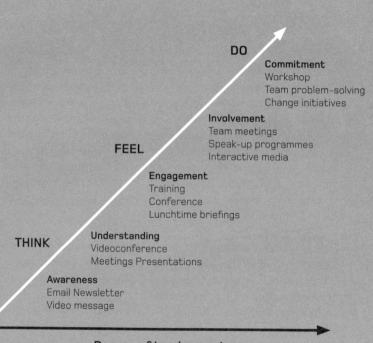

Involvement

'Tell me and I forget, show me and I may remember, involve me and I understand.' Confucius got this right some 2,500 years ago, and it applies just as much today: people understand and learn most from being involved. Organizations have been using the term 'communications and engagement' for some years, but it can feel like something that is *done to* people – it is passive and typically a top-down approach. Involvement is *done with* people. Those who are involved play a more active role, take ownership and implement change. It is a subtle but proven difference.

Effective managers involve team members in working out the best way to achieve objectives. By getting involved in thinking through possibilities and finding solutions, people feel a real sense of ownership. They also understand their role and objectives, and how this fits into the overall picture. Effective forms of involvement may include cross-functional projects, employee forums and staff sounding boards.

PHILOSOPHORUM SINENSIUM
PRINCIPIS
CONFUCII
VITA

UM FU CU, ſeu Confucius quem Sinenſes uti Principem Philoſophiæ ſuæ ſequuntur, & colunt, uulgari vel domeſti- co potius nomine Kieu dictus, cognomento Chum ni, nata- lem habuit ſedem in Regno Lu, quod Regnum hodie Xan- tum dictum; in pago ycu ye territorij Cham pim, quod ad civitatem Kio feu pertinet; hæc autem civitas paret urbi Yen chieu dictæ. Nata eſt anno 21. Imperatoris Lim vam. Fuit hic tertius & vigeſimus è tertia Familiâ, ſeu domo Imperatoria, Cheu dictâ, cycli 10. anno 47. Kem ſin dicto; ſecundâ item & vigeſimo anno Siam vam Regis, qui eâ tempeſtate Regnum Lu obtinebat; idie 19. undecimæ Lunæ Kem cu dictæ; ſub bi ram unicis ſecundum, anno ante Chriſti æram fr. Matre eſt fuit Chiu, è Familia prænobili Yen oriundâ, Patre Xo leam he, qui non ſolùm primi ordinis Magiſtrum, quem geſſit in Regno Sum; ſed prætiis quoque no- bilitatis fuit illuſtris; ſtirpem quippe duxit ſui Chronica Sinenſium te- ſtantur, & tabula genealogica, quæ annalibus inſeritur, perſpicuè doc- et; ex rex ſive penultimo Imperatore Ti ye è, familiâ Xem. Patre natus eſt Confucius Patre ſuo ſeptuagenario, quem adeo triennali Infan- tiæ non amiſit; ſed Matre populi deinde ſuperſtes fuit per annos hunc & viginti, conjuge in monte Tum fam Regni Lu ſepulto. Puer jam ſeve- ris prematurea quædam maturitate, uiro, quem patre ſimilis, cum æqua- libus nunquam riſus eſt luſitare. Oblata edulia non ante delibabat, quam priſca ritu, qui fti reti nuncupabat, cælo venerabundus obtuliſſet. Adhuc annorum quindecim adoleſcens totum ſe dedere cæpit perſcrutari libris evol- vendis, & reſoliis iis, quæ minus utilia videbantur, optima quæque

G g

Meetings

Meetings can take an inordinate amount of time, accomplish little and breed frustration. Some managers call a meeting with little thought for the purpose: a meeting is necessary if something requires discussion; it is not the right forum for imparting information, which can be done via email.

If a meeting is necessary, then a manager should invite the people who can make the best contribution to the discussion. An agenda should be circulated in advance to allow people time to prepare; ideally, this should focus on outcomes rather than topics (i.e. rather than 'June sales figures' it could say 'June sales figures – discuss ideas and agree plan to increase'). Every meeting should start on time, stick to the agenda and finish on time. The chairperson should open by confirming the agenda and finish time. He should allocate a certain period to each agenda item and ensure people stick to the topic. Where a point of view, or additional information, is not relevant, he should state that it will be handled outside the meeting.

Minutes, outputs and notes

It is important to have a record of meetings, but unless it is a formal session, such as a company board meeting that requires proper minutes, simple notes will suffice. The key things to capture and share are: what was decided, what has to be done (actions), who is going to do it and by when.

If a manager is chair of a meeting, or facilitator of a workshop, she should enlist help from someone else to capture the understanding and create the notes. Not only does this avoid bias in interpretation, but it leaves the manager free to ensure there is consensus. Often at a subsequent session someone says: 'I don't remember agreeing to that' – the key is to air misunderstandings and get agreement in the room rather than send out notes, which only a few attendees may read, after the event. One way to do this is to write up relevant points on a flip chart or white board in front of the whole room. Everyone in the meeting can then immediately see what has been agreed, leaving no space for doubt.

Presentations and speeches

Many people have a phobia of public speaking, and it can be far more than just a few butterflies in the stomach – a US survey found that Americans fear public speaking more than death. But it is inevitable that at some stage in a manager's career, she will have to speak in front of an audience.

An effective manager finds out about the audience ahead of the session so she can make the presentation relevant. She knows and owns her content, only agreeing to speak when confident she can be original and authoritative. Repetition and stories will help make the presentation memorable (see page 264); a good speaker will often gain attention by starting with an anecdote. Rehearsal, even in front of a mirror, is a good idea, and 'death by Powerpoint' (simply reading through a large number of overly detailed slides) must be avoided at all costs. The most impactful speeches are those spoken from the heart, rather than ones read from notes. Good speakers rarely talk about themselves; they engage and interact with the audience.

Power of the positive

Always look on the bright side – advice that can be tough, particularly when business is so demanding. Many experts state that a person's feelings about a situation come from perception or attitude. Numerous self-help books espouse the power of positive thinking: some managers read these books while others reject the notion. But there is overwhelming evidence that being positive with a team improves productivity and can be contagious. It helps bring a team together, build relationships and create energy. People want to be with a positive person; they do not want to be around someone who is always negative. A person's attitude determines their confidence, their impact and whether or not they succeed. Negativity wastes energy and time. When a person is focused on the positive it is easier to find solutions, while being emotional or angry can cloud a person's judgement. Winston Churchill once said: 'A pessimist sees the difficulty in every opportunity; an optimist sees the opportunity in every difficulty.' He is likely to have seen the proverbial glass as half full.

Constant change

'I can't wait until things get back to normal.' Employees who say this don't realise that change *is* the new normal. The global economy now moves so fast that organizations must continually improve and change to keep pace. Charities, commercial businesses, education and health providers – in fact, every type of organization – are driven by the world around them. Change is complex, multifaceted and pervasive. Technological improvements, disruptive geopolitics, environmental concerns, societal progress and a burgeoning world population are just some of the factors shaping the 21st century.

Managers used to be able to position change as a project to deal with alongside business as usual. The new reality is that managers must challenge the status quo and 'be the change'. They must be agile and flexible, seeing change as a powerful opportunity and knowing not just what needs changing, but how to deliver it swiftly, effectively and at low cost. Managers who cannot do this are likely to be overtaken by others who can.

Managing change

Given the magnitude and pace of change, how can it be managed? Successful managers view change as a process, albeit a dynamic process with unclear boundaries. It must have a clear direction and sequence to ensure a positive outcome, with steps that may overlap, and may need to be revisited as internal or external factors shift:

1. Define: document rationale for change: why (context), what (scope), where (vision of where the organization wants to be), who (people affected), when (timescales)
2. Plan: create a detailed plan including objectives, scope, stakeholders, people, priorities, milestones
3. Energize the team: assign roles, create understanding, gain commitment, establish working principles
4. Make change happen: change may be in one area, but the interconnections of people, process, technology, structure and technology may produce significant knock-on effects
5. Make change last – sustained change is vital to gaining real benefits for the organization.

Defining

Planning

Energizing
the team

Making change
happen

Making
it last

Change communication

Leading management consultant McKinsey & Company estimates that 70 per cent of change programmes fail to achieve their objective. One of the reasons often cited is lack of communication. An effective manager involved in a major change initiative takes time to understand the context and vision. She then communicates this to her team and makes the transformation meaningful and relevant – she needs to help her team understand the likely impacts.

The message may be hard to deliver if it involves restructuring that affects team members; a good manager states the facts and is not defensive. She allows people to ask questions. Often she will not know the answer; she should say so and give people an expected timeframe to come back to them. Further communication needs to be regular and continuous with the context as the reference point. She cannot just talk about the change, but has to present a role model for the behaviours, values and mindset she expects of her team.

Incremental change

The degree of change will impact how it should be managed, and how employees are likely to react. Managers must evaluate the scale and likely impact of change: the right approach is specific to each initiative, but will also depend on the pace of change in other parts of the organization.

Incremental change is done in small, gradual steps that do not push employees too far out of their current positions and comfort zones. An example might be a cycle of continuous improvement during a food manufacturing process. Bread is often made in batches and a manufacturer may decide to increase the size of each batch to improve process efficiency. The staff working on the line will see little change in their roles, and the manager involved will simply need to explain the extra six loaves per batch as part of the regular team meeting. However, if a change involved new machinery, new skills training or a change in shift patterns, the change would require more careful planning and a different approach.

Transformation

A good way to think about radical change is how American athlete Dick Fosbury fundamentally changed the high jump during the 1960s. By going backwards over the bar, rather than using the traditional scissors or straddle technique, he raised the record and changed the sport. No athlete could compete using the old techniques; the Fosbury Flop was a transformation. Something similar applies in organizations: radical change means a totally new approach, letting go of old ways of working and adopting the new. Examples include: mergers, acquisitions and divestitures; restructuring a business; outsourcing and offshoring; and enterprise software that changes business processes. Suppose a large international company has a number of operations that are organized on a national basis. It then decides to change to an organizational model based on product lines across the globe to reflect customer relationships that are on a similarly global basis. Such a transformation needs careful planning and management to embed the new structure and ways of working.

Resistance

The impact of change on individuals can be turbulent, and experts believe it follows four stages; by understanding this 'change curve', good managers can support successful change:

- Denial: some may not believe the change is real, avoid talking about it and cling to the past. Managers help embed the reality of the change and its effects through discussion
- Resistance: anger and anxiety creep in. Low morale, poor productivity and disruptive behaviour may be manifest. Managers recognize the loss people fear, listen to their concerns and encourage them to make the change work
- Exploration: people understand the significance of their role in the change, leave behind concerns and start to contribute in positive ways. Managers acknowledge change in attitudes and encourage ideas and input
- Commitment: people feel more in control, productivity resumes and energies are channelled into making the change work even better. Managers reward success and acknowledge individual and team accomplishments.

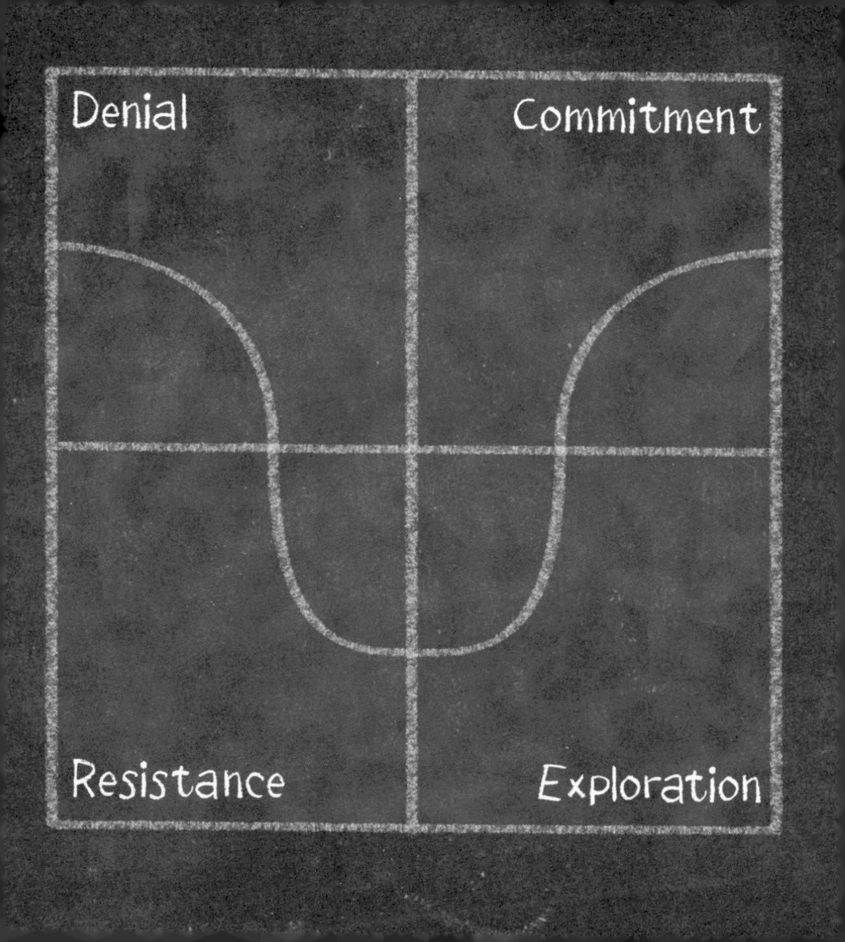
Denial
Commitment
Resistance
Exploration

New beginnings

American business consultant William Bridges believed it is helpful to focus on transition rather than change. Change is an external pressure, while transition is the psychological process people go through. His model proposes three stages of transition:

- Endings – people need to let go of the past before they can embrace the new. Managers must acknowledge people's emotions to avoid resistance, encourage discussion about the past, listen empathetically and emphasize the individual's importance in making change happen
- Neutral zone – in a period of uncertainty, some will cling to the old, while also trying to adapt to the new. Managers should provide regular guidance and feedback; short-term goals and quick wins can help boost morale
- Beginnings – people begin to embrace the new change with energy and enthusiasm. Managers have to celebrate success, reward achievements and sustain the change by realigning personal goals to organizational objectives.

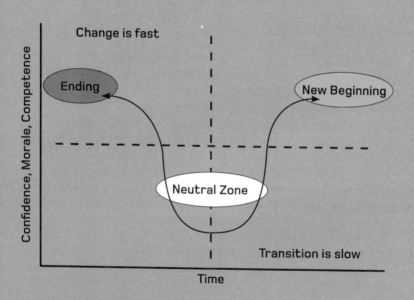

Paranoia

'Success breeds complacency. Complacency breeds failure. Only the paranoid survive.' So claims former Intel CEO Andy Grove. He believes that external forces shape change and that often managers in a business are the last to notice. Some major changes are more like a typhoon. Grove uses the arrival of the internet as an example in his book *Only the Paranoid Survive*: it created a totally new reality, but some organizations and managers failed to recognize its force, or were complacent and did not take action.

An effective manager in any kind of organization must be alert to change. Points of big change are hard to spot, so he must constantly scan the horizon, rather like a ship's watchman looking for a fatal iceberg that could sink the company, or even sink him. Success relies on making sense of the information, and a wise manager is wary of making decisions solely based on data or past events. He knows that business data is relevant to the firm's past alone, and is no predictor of the future.

Innovation

Without new ideas and change, businesses cannot compete and grow. Innovation is not just about creativity, invention and leading-edge products. It is also a mindset. Some people have an innate ability to take risks, overcome obstacles, ask questions and challenge accepted thinking. A supportive culture is vital to enable innovation, and so is a manager's approach. A manager may talk about innovation, but their actions must deliver the same message. Innovative managers:

- Start with customers and find ways to understand their needs
- Encourage ideas in meetings rather than shoot them down
- Allow people freedom – extraordinary ideas can come at unlikely times (that's why companies such as Google have table tennis in the office)
- Encourage team members to develop diverse networks and interact with colleagues in unrelated fields
- Encourage secondments to interdisciplinary projects
- Encourage people to look for connections.

Change skills

A manager has been asked to pick a team for a change project. What skills are needed to make up an effective team? The chosen people may come from different areas of the organization and will bring different strengths, but they will each need to show all or most of these ten key characteristics:

- Vision – ability to see the overall aim of the project and not get side-tracked by trivia or barriers
- Flexibility in attitude and behaviour
- Strong interpersonal skills – verbal communication, influencing and effective presentation
- Ability and willingness to learn
- Good team player
- Respect from peers, stakeholders and business leaders
- Deep understanding of the company culture and dynamics
- Willingness to challenge and be creative – always seeking a better option
- Courage and tenacity
- Willingness to take risks.

WIFM?

'What's in it for me?' When people hear about a change initiative in their workplace, this is the question foremost in their minds. Individuals want to know how it will impact them, rather than the benefits to the organization. Before communicating any change plans, a good manager considers the impact on different stakeholders. A useful way to do this is for the manager to put herself in the shoes of the individual or team and think through this 'WIFM?' question. These impacts can be mapped out and used as the basis for messages in communication.

Often the manager will not know the outcome for individuals in her team because the change has to be worked through; roles and new work methods may not yet be clear. In such situations she has to be honest and spend time listening to individual and team concerns. This can be tough: even though a manager may be impacted by the change herself, she must stay professional and not engage in conversations about her own uncertainty.

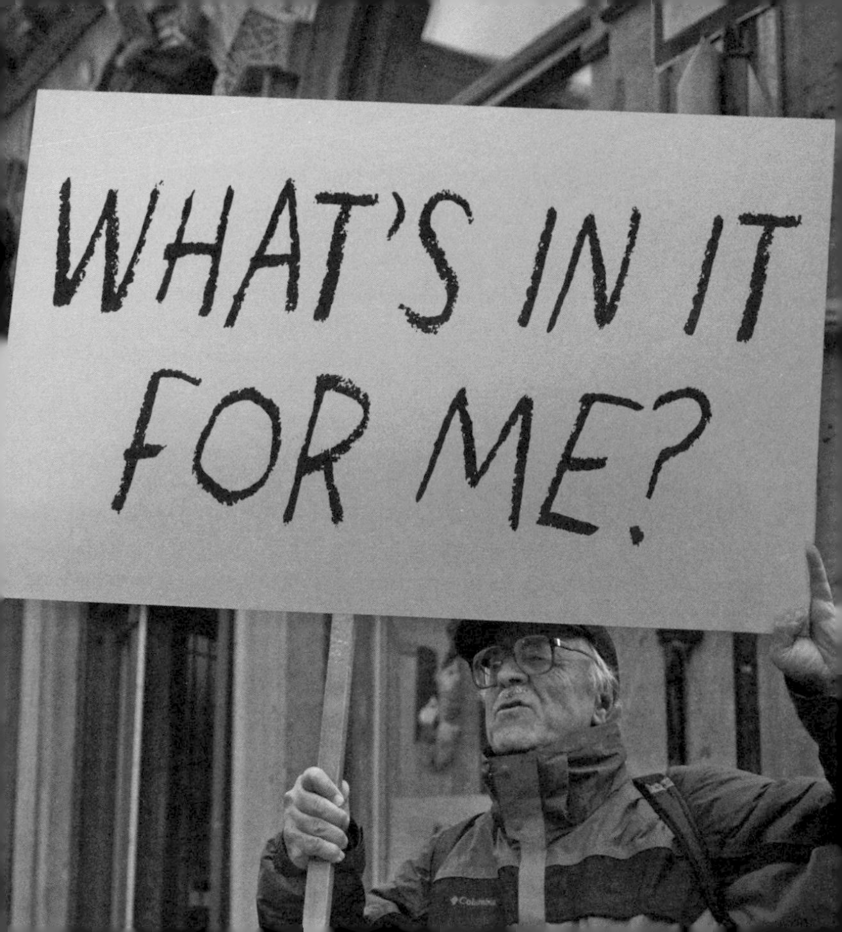
WHAT'S IN IT
FOR ME?

Gurus and theories

Management theory began in the late 19th century when American engineer and steelworks foreman Frederick W. Taylor realised that the way people were managed and organized could improve efficiency. So-called scientific management theory grew, based on the idea of 'one right way': it included time and motion studies, developed by Frank Gilbreth. The human factor was introduced by his wife, American psychologist Lillian Gilbreth, who saw motivation and other psychological factors as important.

In the 1950s, psychologists such as Abraham Maslow and Frederick Herzberg argued that people were motivated by more than money, and around the same time, Peter Drucker, often described as *the* management guru, introduced the 'knowledge worker' concept, recognizing that people are not simply factors of production but use information in their work. Management theories have now gone full circle from Taylor's ideas; and today mostly concern people taking responsibility for continuous learning and improvement, with decision-making pushed down through the organization.

Gods of Management

In his 1979 book *Gods of Management*, author Charles Handy used ancient Greek gods to create a classification of four management cultures based on the power of individuals' roles and functions in the organization. This can offer a useful way to help identify an organization's dominant culture.

Zeus – club culture: Power is concentrated in the hands of the top person, with control through personal contacts rather than procedures (e.g. investment banks and brokerage firms).

Apollo – role culture: Power is hierarchical and clearly defined by job descriptions, with decision-making at the top of the bureaucracy (e.g. life insurance companies).

Athens – task culture: Power is derived from the expertise required to complete a task or project, with decision-making through meritocracies (e.g. advertising agencies).

Dionysius – existential culture: Organizations exist for individuals to achieve their goals, with decision-making by consent of the professionals (e.g. universities and professional service firms).

In search of excellence

In their 1982 book *In Search of Excellence*, Tom Peters (right) and Bob Waterman looked at America's best-run companies and identified eight key attributes of effective organizations:

- A bias for action – active decision-making and learning from mistakes
- Get and stay close to the customer – an obsession with quality, reliability and customer service
- A mindset of autonomy and entrepreneurship – innovation is pushed to the front line and risk-taking encouraged
- Productivity through people – ideas and actions from rank and file employees are the main source of productivity gains
- Hands-on, value-driven – leaders are highly visible and close to the front line, values are clear and taken seriously
- Stick to the knitting – company sticks to a business it knows
- Simple form, lean staff – flat organization with a clear reporting structure
- Simultaneously loose and tight – employees adhere strictly to company values, but can tackle daily tasks their own way.

Learning styles

David Kolb, in his 1984 book *Experiential Learning*, described a four-stage learning cycle: concrete experience (CE) is followed by reflective observation (RO), we then apply theories to the experience in abstract conceptualization (AC), and go on to modify our experiences in active experimentation (AE). In this model, learning styles/preferences fall into four categories:

- Diverging (feeling and watching – CE/RO): able to look at things from different perspectives. Prefers to work in groups, keep an open mind and receive feedback
- Assimilating (watching and thinking – RO/AC): uses a logical approach; concepts more important than people. Prefers readings, lectures and exploring analytical models
- Converging (thinking and doing – AC/AE): able to solve problems and find solutions. Prefers to experiment with new ideas and work with practical applications
- Accommodating (doing and feeling – AE/CE): 'hands-on', relying on intuition rather than logic. Prefers to rely on others for information and work in teams to complete tasks.

Kolb's learning styles

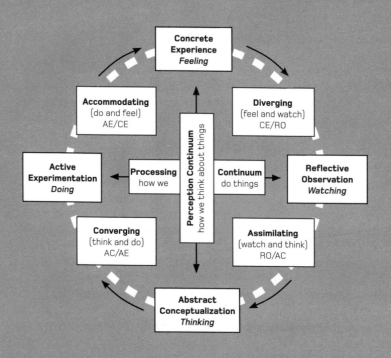

Motivational theory

American psychologist Frederick Herzberg introduced the two-factor theory of work motivation in 1959. His theory states that two different sets of factors – 'hygiene factors' and 'motivation factors' affect job satisfaction and dissatisfaction, and these are not on the same continuum. Hygiene factors, which are about the process of doing a job, do not motivate people, but can cause dissatisfaction if they are absent. Motivation factors lead to positive job attitudes, but are rarely the cause of dissatisfaction.

Both hygiene and motivation factors need to be considered by a manager in order to ensure employees are satisfied and motivated in their roles. The hygiene factors, once satisfied, must simply be maintained, but motivation factors must be continually addressed. One of the important concepts that Herzberg put forward from this work was that of job enrichment, where an employee should be given additional tasks, more involvement and greater interaction in their role.

Improving these factors
decreases job dissatisfaction

Hygiene factors	Motivation
Supervision	Achievement
Relationship with manager	Recognition
Work conditions	The work itself
Salary	Responsibilities
Relationship with colleagues	Advancement
	Personal growth

Improving these factors
increases job satisfaction

Hierarchy of needs

Even though it is more than 70 years since Abraham Maslow first put forward his *Theory of Human Motivation*, his thinking still resonates in modern management theory. In particular, Maslow introduced the concept of a hierarchy of needs. Humans are motivated by needs and once we have satisfied a basic need, we move up to a higher one. At the bottom of this pyramid are physiological needs such as food and water, while at the top are growth needs where we seek 'self-actualization'.

Applying this theory to the workplace saw managers begin to move from simple transactional contracts with staff (paying wages for defined tasks), to more complex psychological contracts in which organizations offer opportunities to develop and grow but have higher expectations in return. Today the concept is used by managers as the basis to understand and build on people's different needs. Some people will be more interested in basic needs such as money, and others in higher needs such as development and promotion.

SELF-ACTUALIZATION
(achieving individual potential)

ESTEEM
(from self and from others)

BELONGING
(love, affection, being part of a group)

SAFETY
(shelter, removal from danger)

PHYSIOLOGICAL
(health, food, sleep)

X Y Theory

The idea of two fundamentally different management styles based on assumptions about people and behaviours originates with American academic Douglas McGregor, and was inspired by Maslow's hierarchy of needs. 'Theory X' assumes that individuals dislike work and responsibility and must be coerced to perform. This laziness demands an authoritarian style where the emphasis is on productivity; managers have to intervene regularly, there is little delegation, the work is repetitive and control is centralized. 'Theory Y' assumes that individuals *like* work and responsibility, are creative and are keen to self-direct. This requires a participative, decentralized style of management: work tends to be organized around broad areas of skill or knowledge, and managers involve people in decision-making but retain power to implement decisions. McGregor urged companies to adopt Theory Y as he believed this would motivate human beings to the highest levels of achievement. Theory X merely satisfies their lower-level physical needs and means that people are likely to be less productive.

THEORY X

Management

Theory X – authoritarian, repressive style. Tight control, no development. Produces limited, depressed culture.

Staff

THEORY Y

Staff

Theory Y – liberating and developmental. Control, achievement and continuous improvement, achieved by enabling, empowering and giving responsibility.

Management

Seven S model

In the early 1980s, McKinsey consultants Tom Peters and Bob Waterman came up with a model of organizational effectiveness that has endured. Its basic premise is that for an organization to be successful, seven internal aspects need to be aligned. These are divided into hard and soft elements. Hard elements are easier to define and influence:

- Strategy: the plan devised to maintain and build competitive advantage over competition
- Structure: the way the organization is structured and reporting lines
- Systems: the daily activities and procedures that staff members engage in to get the job done

Soft elements are less tangible and rooted in company culture:

- Style: the approach to leadership adopted
- Staff: the employees and their capabilities
- Skills: the abilities and competencies of the workforce
- Shared values: the corporate culture and general work ethic (placed at the centre to indicate its pivotal role).

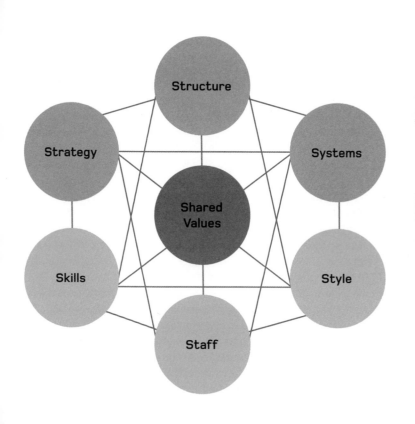

Management by objectives

The idea of Management by Objectives (MBO) became popular in the 1960s. Today it seems obvious that managers need clear goals, but Peter Drucker argued that events take over and it is easy to lose sight of the original purpose.

The core of MBO is planning so that people are proactive, not merely reacting to problems. Employees set measurable personal objectives, and effective coordination ensures that these all contribute to the overall organizational goal. Objectives are recorded annually and monitored by managers, with rewards based upon achievement of objectives. The advantages of MBO include a clear plan to achieve the organization's goals, proactive behaviour and a disciplined approach. Goals are measurable, progress is transparent and organizations can prepare for obstacles. Morale can be high if the process is well managed, but critics of MBO believe that it can become mechanical, with the setting of goals becoming the organization's primary activity. Rapid change can also make the goals irrelevant.

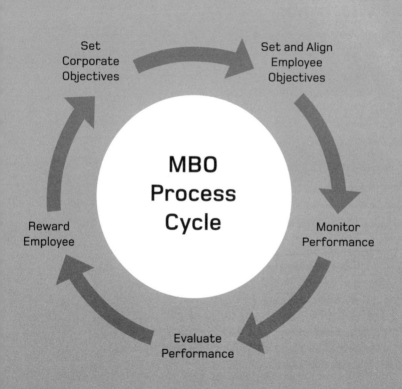

Learning organizations

The ideas of American scientist and academic Peter Senge on organizational development have changed the way businesses approach learning. Senge studied how learning was shared in organizations and how learning capacity was built, and identified five 'learning disciplines':

- Shared vision – common understanding, commitment and aspirations
- Mental models – beliefs, values and assumptions that determine the way people think and act
- Personal mastery – self-awareness and understanding of the impact individual behaviour has on others
- Systems thinking – seeing complex interactions rather than simplistic linear cause-effect chains
- Team learning – sharing insights, experience and skills.

Senge further outlines an ideal 'learning organization', where 'people continually expand their capacity to create the results they truly desire ... where collective aspiration is set free and where people are continually learning how to learn together.'

Pareto principle

At the start of the 20th century, Italian economist Vilfredo Pareto noticed that 80 per cent of Italy's wealth belonged to 20 per cent of the population. Pareto developed the idea that the 80:20 proportional split is often seen. For example, in business: 80 per cent of revenue comes from 20 per cent of products, 80 per cent of profit comes from 20 per cent of customers, and 80 per cent of results come from 20 per cent of activities.

The 80:20 rule can help a manager with prioritization. A successful manager identifies and focuses on the 20 per cent of activities that will deliver the maximum results. This is vital to understand how to prioritize effectively. Suppose a manager has numerous issues on his desk – he lists the problems and their causes. It is likely that when he does this, 80 per cent of the problems will be caused by 20 per cent of the issues. The manager can then choose to work on those causes so he solves the majority of his problems.

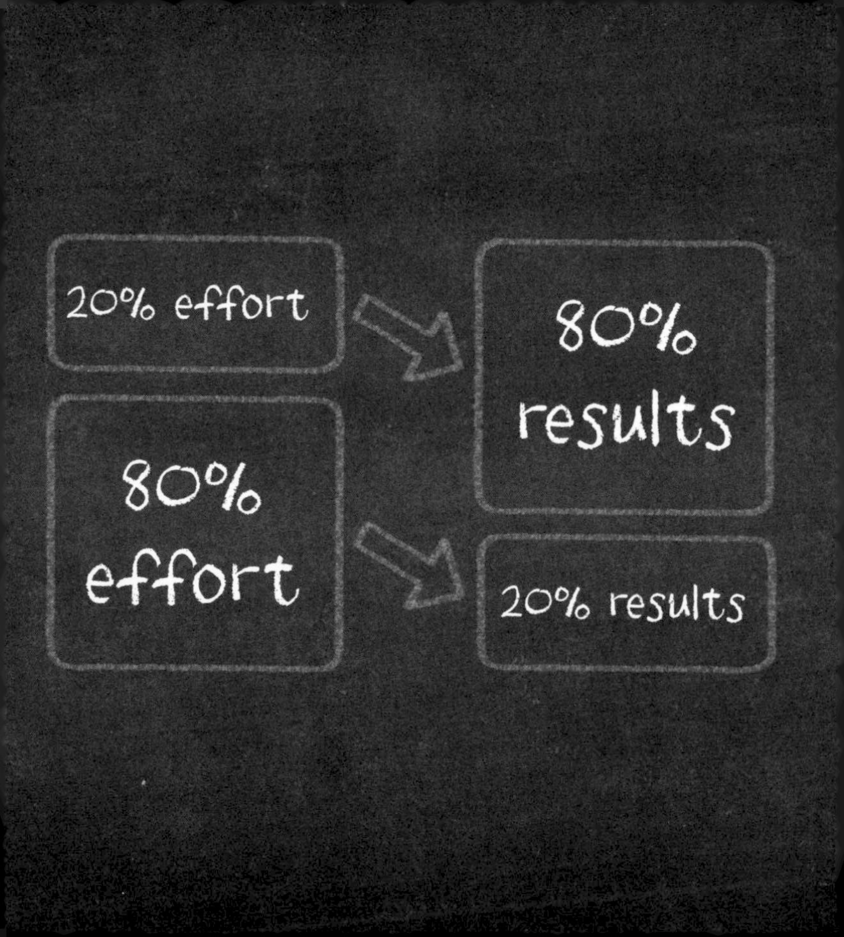
20% effort
80% effort
80% results
20% results

Thinking outside the box

Thinking outside the box has become something of a cliché but, although management problems do not come in boxes, the concept remains important. It is a metaphor for thinking differently – looking beyond real or perceived boundaries to consider unobvious ideas or solutions. The most apparent answer may not always be the best one.

The notion of a box is believed to come from the 'nine dots' puzzle. This puzzle was popularized by consultants in the 1980s, as organizations looked to improve creativity and innovation, but the concept is believed to be much older. The puzzle is an intellectual challenge because people are asked to connect nine dots by drawing four, continuous, straight lines that pass through each dot, and never lift the pencil from the paper. It seems impossible because people perceive an imaginary boundary. The only way to solve the puzzle is to extend the pencil lines outside the area/box defined by the dots, as shown opposite.

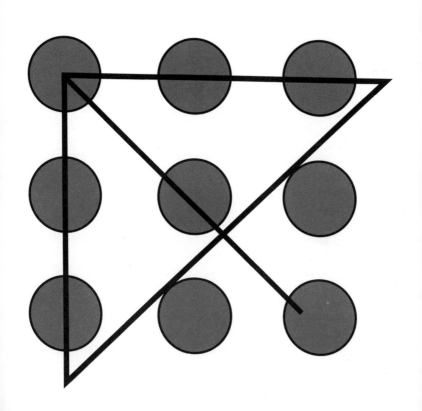

Balanced scorecard

Organizations used to measure success in financial terms alone, but in the 1990s business gurus Robert Kaplan and David Norton developed the 'balanced scorecard' concept, adding non-financial performance measures to traditional metrics to give managers a more balanced view of performance. This concept enables organizations to take strategy from a passive document to a plan that can be put into action: the idea is that managers can set and review measures around both internal processes and external outcomes, continuously improving performance and results. The balanced scorecard views an organization from four perspectives:

- Learning and growth – employee training and cultural issues related to individual and corporate self-improvement
- Business process perspective – internal business processes
- Customer perspective – customer focus and customer satisfaction
- Financial perspective – finance and financially related data, such as risk assessment and cost-benefit information.

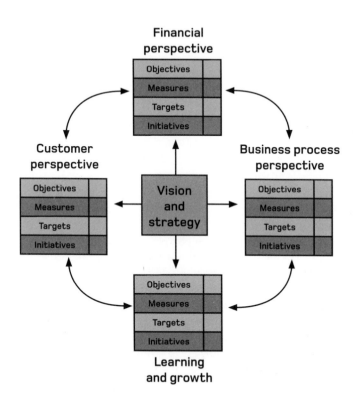

Opportunity cost

Taking one course of action often means that another cannot be taken, and opportunity cost is the cost of that missed opportunity or the value foregone. The concept is often used in economics, and was first coined by Austrian economist Friedrich von Wieser in 1914. Decisions in business are often about how to use scarce resources, and this concept is useful where managers have to choose one option over another. Opportunity cost is typically a monetary definition (it might refer, for example, to profit that could have been earned if limited finance or assets were used in a different way), but it may also include other considerations such as people or production output.

The finance team is unlikely to consider opportunity cost as it is always hypothetical and intangible, but managers should think through its implications when faced with a choice of actions, or indeed taking any action. Suppose they are offered an exclusive deal with one retailer for the firm's products. What other retail opportunities might this close down?

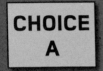

CHOICE
A

CHOICE
B

Value chain

One way to think about business is that organizations take inputs and convert them into outputs with a greater value than the combined cost of inputs and production. Michael Porter of Harvard Business School introduced the concept of the value chain in 1985, envisaging an organization as carrying out a set of activities to create value for its customers. How the activities are carried out determines the cost, and therefore the amount of profit. The value chain is based on a process view of activities that change inputs into outputs. Using this viewpoint, Porter describes a chain of activities common to all businesses, dividing them into primary and support activities. Primary activities are: inbound logistics, operations, outbound logistics, marketing and sales, and service. Support activities are: procurement, human resource management, technological development and infrastructure. Effective managers understand how their company creates value, and look for ways to add more value, as this is a critical element in developing a competitive strategy.

Firm Infrastructure

Human Resource Management

Technology Development

Procurement

Support Activities

Margin

Margin

Inbound Logistics | Operations | Outbound Logistics | Marketing & Sales | Service

Primary Activities

Right first time

'We had a fundamental belief that doing it right the first time was going to be easier than having to go back and fix it. And I cannot say strongly enough that the repercussions of that attitude are staggering. I've seen them again and again throughout my business life.' That was the view of Steve Jobs, the man who built Apple into a multibillion dollar business.

The idea of getting something right first time came out of Japanese manufacturing industry in the 1970s, with its pursuit of quality and zero defects. The notion seems obvious today: defect prevention is more advantageous and cost effective than defect detection and associated reworking. Right first time does not have specific steps; rather it is a philosophy that can be applied to any business, industry or situation. It has been embraced by manufacturing, and successful managers carry it through to other areas – ensuring, for example, they use the correct data for analysis, involve the right stakeholders and have robust version control on documents.

10/10
all correct

Kaizen

The *Kaizen* philosophy came out of the Japanese manufacturing industry after the Second World War and inspired its success by producing high quality at low cost. It is an approach rather than a specific tool set, so can be applied to any team or organization. *Kaizen* means 'good change', and its fundamental idea is that all employees are responsible for continuous improvement. *Kaizen* is based on making small changes on a regular basis: always improving productivity, safety and effectiveness while reducing waste. It is not limited to manufacture, but to any area where improvements can be made. *Kaizen* encompasses many successful components of Japanese business: quality circles, automation, suggestion systems, just-in-time delivery, *kanban* (scheduling system for lean production) and '5S' (sort, straighten, shine, standardize and sustain). If Western philosophy may be summarized as: 'if it ain't broke, don't fix it', the *Kaizen* approach is 'do it better, make it better, improve it even if it isn't broken, because if we don't, we can't compete with those who do'.

kai

Zen

Change

Good

Benchmarking

Benchmarking is a way of identifying best practice and comparing performance – understanding who sets the standard, what that standard is and why they are the best. It can take place internally, where similar operations within the organization are compared; externally with competitors, where companies in the same field are compared; or even externally to companies in other fields. In the last case, Formula 1 is often used, because of its focus on high performance and winning.

Benchmarking can apply to almost any aspect of business, not just business processes. Suppose a manager wants to understand why competitors continually attract better talent. He may carry out a benchmark exercise to understand the pay and benefits packages offered across the sector. The idea would be to examine how other firms attract better people, understand the packages firms offer, compare his own firm's pay and benefits packages to those of the companies analysed, and determine whether and how to close the gap, if any exists.

PEST analysis

PEST analysis is used to look at the political, economic, social and technological changes that are likely to shape any business environment. That environment could be a new or existing market, a region or a country. It is a useful tool for a manager to understand the big forces operating in the chosen market and how to respond. PEST can be used to structure a brainstorm, asking questions that relate to the specific business under the four headings. Benefits include:

- Spotting business opportunities and highlighting potential threats
- Focusing on projects that are more likely to succeed
- Revealing the direction of change within the business environment; this helps shape activities so that the business moves with the change, rather than against it
- Removing unconscious assumptions when considering a new market by creating an objective view of its environment
- Analysis can be extended to take in social, demographic, legal or ethical changes.

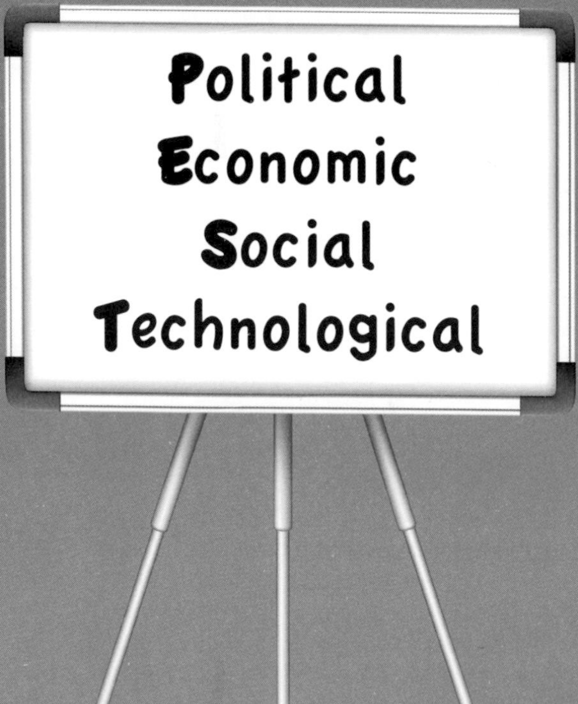
Political
Economic
Social
Technological

SWOT analysis

SWOT analysis is the simple idea of evaluating strengths, weaknesses, opportunities and threats. The starting point is always an objective, and the tool is used to identify internal and external factors that will have a positive or negative impact on that objective. SWOT can be used in many different situations: in a personal context, for day-to-day business operations such as understanding competitors, or when considering a one-off project. Managers can also use it in a group environment as a way of engaging people in strategy formulation. Its most effective use is to ask open questions, such as:

- Strengths: what are we best at? What intellectual property, skills and financial resources do we have?
- Weaknesses: what are we not good at? What connections and alliances should we have, but don't?
- Opportunities: what external changes can we exploit? Do our competitors have weaknesses we can benefit from?
- Threats: what might our competitors do that would affect us? What social trends might threaten us?

Swot Analysis

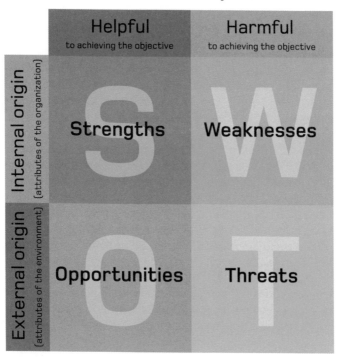

Critical path analysis

Critical path analysis (CPA) is a useful tool for scheduling activities, and is increasingly used in large-scale, complex projects. The essential idea is that some activities are dependent on others, and so have to be completed in the right sequence, while others are independent and since they are not 'time critical', they may be undertaken in parallel.

Setting out activities as a critical path enables a clear picture of the project from start to finish, and allows the planning and optimization of resources. For example, it is possible to plan and group activities that require hiring a major piece of expensive equipment in order to minimize costs. Typically the critical path has no spare time or slack – if there is a delay in any of the activities on the path, the whole project risks being delayed unless the manager takes action. Understanding the principles is important, although today firms typically use software packages such as Microsoft Project® to draw up and manage critical paths for projects.

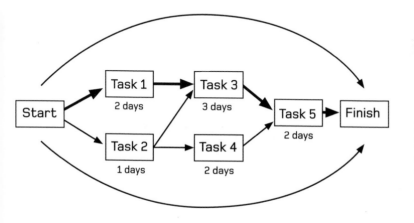

This simplified analysis shows that although the actual project activities would take 10 days in total, the critical path is only 7 days. Tasks 1 and 2 can be undertaken in parallel, as can Tasks 3 and 4.

Six thinking hats

Edward de Bono, one of the leading authorities on thinking skills, developed a method known as Six Thinking Hats®. The idea is for people to mentally wear and switch hats that compartmentalize thinking into specific roles. This forces people to move outside their typical thinking style to gain a more rounded view of a situation. The hats are symbolized by colours:

- Facts (white hat): known or needed information; think about data and facts
- Optimism (yellow hat): assume a bright outlook to explore the positives and probe for value and benefit
- Pessimism (black hat): look at why something may not work, revealing difficulties and dangers
- Feelings (red hat): what are your hunches and intuitions; express emotions and feelings, or use gut instinct
- Creativity (green hat): consider possibilities, alternatives and new ideas
- Control (blue hat): the mechanism used to manage the thinking process. Worn by the person chairing the meeting.

Facts

Optimism

Pessimism

Feelings

Creativity

Control

Force field analysis

Created by German-American social psychologist Kurt Lewin in the 1940s, force field analysis is a useful tool for a manager to support decision-making, since it looks at both positive forces for change towards a goal (driving forces) and forces against change (restraining forces). Lewin's idea was that where there is equilibrium between forces there is stability and no change will occur. When driving forces exceed restraining forces change is more likely. The concept can be applied to any business objective or organizational change.

Ideally a manager should work with a small group to discuss a potential change, which should be written as a goal; for example, achieve operational savings by reducing the number of permanent staff. The team should use a flipchart or whiteboard and write up the forces for change on the left and forces against change to the right. The forces should be sorted into common themes and scored according to their strength, from one (weak) to five (strong).

FORCE FIELD ANALYSIS - KURT LEWIN

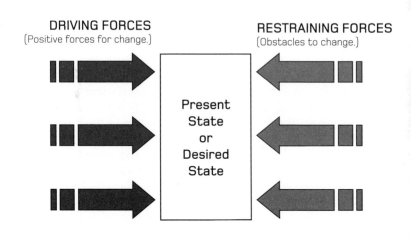

DRIVING FORCES
(Positive forces for change.)

RESTRAINING FORCES
(Obstacles to change.)

Present
State
or
Desired
State

Game changers

Just as management gurus have an impact on the way people are managed, so business leaders can also wield significant influence, as others seek to understand and emulate their style and ideas. Often such game changers are the first to bring an idea to market or to use a particular management approach.

One of the great first-movers was Richard Arkwright, inventor of the modern factory. He devised a complete mechanized system for the spinning of cotton yarn in the mid-18th century. Even though he eventually lost control of the technology, he had the advantage of a head-start on his competitors. Henry Ford did the same with his idea of the assembly line, copied from watchmakers and meat packers. Such pioneers are prepared to take risks. From Anita Roddick, with her idea of ethical and sustainable products at the Body Shop, to Apple's Steve Jobs who saw technology as a way to revolutionize communication and entertainment, these game changers have not only transformed business but also the way we live.

Jeff Bezos – customer focus

'We see our customers as invited guests to a party, and we are the hosts. It's our job every day to make every important aspect of the customer experience a little bit better.'

As founder, chairman and CEO of online retail giant Amazon, Jeff Bezos puts himself in the shoes of the customer. He spotted the opportunity of the burgeoning internet in 1994 and saw that customers would want to buy anything and everything via the internet rather than from physical stores. With that vision of eCommerce, he set up his fledgling company in his garage and began developing the necessary software for an online retail business. Amazon was launched in July 1995, initially selling books, and became an instant success. He went on to expand into CDs, and then later to clothes, toys and electronics through retail partnerships. His vision led to the concept of the eBook, with the launch of Kindle in 2007. Today, Amazon has annual revenues of more than $89 billion.

Richard Branson — enjoyment

'A business has to be involving, it has to be fun, and it has to exercise your creative instincts.'

Virgin Group founder Richard Branson dropped out of school at 16 and started a mail-order record company in order to help fund his newly launched magazine *Student*. He opened his first record store on London's Oxford Street in 1971 and was a millionaire by the age of 23. Today Virgin Group holds more than 200 companies in more than 30 countries, including airlines, hotels, mobile-phone companies, banks and even space tourism. Branson has a reputation for doing things differently and has involved himself in world-record attempts, dressing up as a bride and other stunts to launch his different companies. He puts employees first, customers second and shareholders third. He believes that if people are happy in their job they will serve customers better and the business will be a success. He also collects feedback from employees to ensure they enjoy working for Virgin.

Michael Dell—never accept the status quo

'Celebrate for a nanosecond. Then move on.'

The founder and CEO of Dell Inc. is renowned for his belief that the status quo is never good enough. Michael Dell seeks constant improvement, believing that everything the company does can be changed and that people can learn from mistakes. He began building computers in his room at the University of Texas for students he knew, and helped launch the personal computer revolution in the 1980s with the creation of the Dell Computer Corporation. Using a direct-sales model, he bypassed the middleman and so delivered cheaper prices and strong customer support well before the arrival of the internet. Dell soon dropped out of education to focus on his business. His company built computers to order, rather than holding stocks of finished goods, which has benefits for the supply chain and manufacturing. Within eight years, he had become the youngest CEO of a Fortune 500 company.

Walt Disney – process and quality

'Think of process as a railroad engine. If the engine does not run properly, it does not matter how friendly the conductor acts … the train will still not move. Process is the engine of quality service.'

Animator and entrepreneur Walt Disney (1901–66) created many cartoon characters starting with Mickey Mouse. From these characters came magical experiences, and yet there is no magic involved in Disney's hugely successful theme parks – rather a rigorous focus on process and quality. Walt Disney viewed his theme parks almost as factories that produced delight and entertainment. He believed that people want a consistent quality experience and he could deliver this by establishing exacting processes and then repeating them at scale. He was obsessed with detail because he saw his parks as incomplete products that could always be improved, and would visit incognito to understand the experience from a customer's perspective.

Henry Ford –
focus on solutions

'If you think you can do a thing or think you can't do a thing, you're right.'

When cars appeared at the start of the 20th century, they were exclusively for the rich. In founding the Ford Motor Company, Henry Ford (1863–1947) pursued his idea that cars could be for everyone. Ford did not invent the car, but he brought them to the masses through the success of his affordable Model T. And despite the widespread misconception, Ford did not invent the assembly line either. However, he did identify it as the solution to how he could make cars quicker and cheaper. When he faced high absenteeism and labour turnover, caused by the monotony of the assembly line, his solution was to double the wage and cut daily working hours. He worked out that this would help him produce more cars in less time because people would work better. Ford's vision helped create a middle class in the US – one marked by urbanization, rising wages and free time for workers to spend their pay.

Soichiro Honda — tenacity

'Success represents the 1% of your work which results from the 99% that is called failure.'

Soichiro Honda (1906–91) learnt mechanics in his father's bicycle repair shop and from an early age was fascinated by cars. Despite numerous setbacks, he never accepted failure and built one of the world's largest automobile companies. Honda's first business venture was a company to make piston rings, which he later sold to Toyota. When construction materials were in short supply because of the Second World War and he needed to build a factory, he invented a concrete-making process. Equally undeterred by the short supply of steel, he made ingenious use of gas cans discarded from US bomber aircraft. After the war, there was no fuel for cars, and so Honda invented a tiny bicycle engine. He set up the company that went on to make mopeds and the best-selling motorcycles in the world. Cars and aircraft engines followed, all with a reputation for Japanese quality.

Steve Jobs — innovation

'Creativity is just connecting things. When you ask creative people how they did something, they feel a little guilty because they didn't really do it, they just saw something. It seemed obvious to them.'

Throughout a career as co-founder, chairman and CEO of Apple Inc., Steve Jobs (1955–2011) revolutionized the fields of computers, telecommunications, entertainment, music and retail. He started Apple Computers with Steve Wozniak in 1976 after dropping out of college at the age of just 21. Jobs had learned a love of electronics from his adopted father, and they started out in the family garage. Their small, user-friendly computers sold fast and Apple went public in 1980 – in 2014, it became the world's biggest ever company. Jobs used experiences to inspire his best ideas and said that he did not always know where the dots would connect. One example was that he had studied calligraphy in college – this led to his interest in typography and the simplicity of Macintosh fonts.

Indra Nooyi – authentic leadership

'At the end of the day, don't forget that you're a person, don't forget you're a mother, don't forget you're a wife, don't forget you're a daughter.'

When Indra Nooyi moved to the US from her native Mumbai to attend Yale in 1978, she had to wear her sari because she could not afford to buy Western clothes. She is now one of the world's leading businesswomen as chair and CEO of the global snack food company PepsiCo.

Nooyi is seen as approachable and makes time to speak to employees. She also finds time for family life with her husband and two daughters. Nooyi states that she has built a successful career because she has always taken on tough assignments and that people would not have noticed if she had done easy jobs well. Under her leadership, PepsiCo has reshaped its business, disposing of its restaurant division and acquiring big brands such as Tropicana and Quaker.

Anita Roddick – ethical business

'I want to work for a company that contributes to and is part of the community. I want something not just to invest in. I want something to believe in.'

From her first Body Shop store in Brighton in 1976, Anita Roddick (1942–2007) went on to create a global business uniquely associated with social responsibility, respect for human rights, the environment, animal protection and fair community trade. The green movement was in its infancy and Roddick firmly believed that business had the power to do good. Her ideas came from rural communities on her world travels, and from her thrifty Italian immigrant mother. The store opened with products with only natural ingredients, no animal testing and refillable bottles. The brand was aligned with a number of ethical causes - it became a trailblazer of fair trade, and the first to develop relationships with communities in return for natural ingredients. Other companies, in fields from cosmetics to food, have since had to follow suit.

Jack Welch – empowerment

'Giving people self-confidence is by far the most important thing that I can do. Because then they will act.'

Jack Welch joined the US General Electric (GE) corporation as a junior engineer in 1960, and rose to become the company's youngest vice president and later its youngest CEO and chairman. His no-nonsense, dynamic management style has been copied across the globe. Welch restructured GE, sold off unprofitable businesses and brought in a process focus with the Six Sigma programme. Although he was known for a ruthless drive for efficiency, he was not remote. Knowing that employee morale affected productivity, he communicated regularly, even sending personal notes to engender a sense of pride in the job. He worked hard to rid GE of its bureaucracy, dispensing with formal management meetings and empowering managers to make quick decisions in response to the pace of competition. When he retired in 2001, GE was the most valuable company in the world.

Technology

Technology has enabled us to capture and store vast amounts of data. No one really knows how much data is available today because the volume is growing so fast. Data is always 'correct' by its nature; it is simply facts such as words, numbers and dates, but lacks context. For example, personal data includes an individual's date and place of birth, and even their DNA. A company's data may include a list of customers.

Information and data are different: information puts data into context or structure. For example, sorting the customer data into ages, geographic regions or spend value would create useful information that a company could use as the basis for decisions. Spreadsheets are the most common way of doing this. However, managers need to be aware that the information in the spreadsheet captures data at a single point in time and as such is a snapshot. Understanding the difference between data and information, and using their own knowledge and experience, helps managers make better decisions.

Business intelligence

Computers can be programmed to make simple decisions based on data; for example, to pay a person's weekly wage based on the hours they have worked. But such systems can only be as good as the rules programmed, and cannot deal with the unexpected. For example, expert systems such as automatic pilots in airplanes can handle volumes of data, but the pilot's own judgement is still needed for some decisions.

Modern technology allows us to develop techniques and tools that transform raw data into meaningful information for the purpose of business analysis. Called business intelligence, these technologies can handle vast amounts of unstructured data and allow managers to interpret it more easily. Data mining tools, for example, can find patterns in large databases. One area where these techniques are used is for analysis of social media. The sheer scale would make it impossible for humans to read but computers can carry out initial analysis, allowing managers to use their knowledge to evaluate further.

Technical platforms

A computer platform consists of hardware (a computer) and software (its operating system, such as Windows® or Mac OS®). It is the base on which other applications, processes and technologies are developed. Platforms are an important concept because they allow massive companies to draw consumers into their world. Google, for example, has integrated features such as YouTube™, Maps, GMail™, and numerous others, into what was essentially just a search engine.

Such large organizations are reshaping business models: in the 20th century a traditional business produced one or more related products or services, then used marketing to attract customers. Now organizations entice consumers into their 'ecosystem', encouraging them to be both part of a community and a wider world. For example, Facebook now has 1.39 billion users. Innovative managers understand the concept of platforms, consider what their customers need and work out how such platforms can be used to their advantage.

Enterprise resource planning

Enterprise resource planning (ERP) is a way for organizations to use technology to integrate core business processes, such as taking sales orders, scheduling manufacturing, ordering raw materials, issuing invoices and paying employees. Many ERP systems are a suite of integrated applications sharing a common database. Increasingly, such systems are considered vital – the integration they offer makes business processes faster, more efficient and less prone to error, while the real-time information they provide supports better decision-making. The two largest ERP systems today are SAP and Oracle.

The automation of many aspects of business frees people from mundane repetitive tasks, but the introduction of ERP in many organizations is not always straightforward: more than just a new technology, it requires a new way of working, changing people's roles and often reshaping culture. Many organizations use change management and communication alongside the technical implementation to secure its benefits.

Customer relationship management

Customers today drive businesses, and managing that relationship is crucial, no matter what the size of business. The traditional approach was based on a transaction at the point of sale, and typically a single point of contact, such as a salesman. Now organizations have multiple 'touch points' with customers and aim for a deeper relationship (see page 88).

Customer relationship management (CRM) systems enable an organization to manage all its different customer interactions at levels from HR to finance. The simplest systems manage contacts with individual customers, integrating email communication, documents and scheduling jobs for small businesses. Larger and more complex systems may form part of ERP (see page 374), which organizes, automates and synchronizes customer processes, sales, marketing, customer service and technical support. CRM data and information can help develop better strategies for managing existing and potential customers and improving profitability.

Business processes

Economist Adam Smith was the first to envisage business processes in 1776, when he broke the making of a pin into different tasks. Since then, there have been numerous approaches to making processes more efficient – from time and motion studies in the early 20th century to business process engineering in the 1990s. Numerous ways of depicting processes have also been used, from flowcharts to Gantt charts.

Considering process, rather than function, is a way to look at a chain of events in an organization when, for example, a customer orders a product. How does the order flow through the company and the product arrive with the customer? An organization can model this process, analyse it and look at how to improve it. There may be any number of objectives for doing this, including speed to market, improved quality, reduced costs, less wastage or better labour utilization. Business process modelling (BPM) is carried out where a technology project is going to automate the steps in a process.

Disruptive technology

In 1997, Harvard Business School professor Clayton Christensen suggested that all new technology could be classified as either sustaining or disruptive. Sustaining technology makes incremental improvements to already established technology, and is typically the area in which most companies work. Disruptive technology displaces established technology or delivers a groundbreaking product that can create a completely new industry. It has the potential to overturn the status quo, alter the way people live and work, and change accepted business models. Previous examples include the worldwide web, email and laptop/mobile computing. On the horizon are self-driving cars, 3D printing and advanced robotics.

Ambitious managers aim to consider the role technology has to play in any strategy. The challenge is to make sense of relentless innovations, determining which might alter the social and business landscape, and identifying those which represent opportunities or threats.

Cloud computing

The delivery of on-demand computing resources via the internet means that consumers or businesses no longer need to buy software for an individual computer – perhaps the best known examples are web-based email services such as Hotmail or Gmail. Cloud computing is useful for business as it can remove costs, increase flexibility and allow instant access to information. There are three types of clouds: public (accessible to any subscriber); private (accessible by, say, a business and its customers); or a hybrid that combines the two. Organizations look to cloud providers for three levels of service:

- Software as a Service (SaaS) – provider gives access to required applications via the internet
- Platform as a Service (PaaS) – provider gives access to components required to develop and operate applications over the internet
- Infrastructure as a Service (IaaS) – the business completely outsources storage and resources, such as hardware and software to the provider on a pay-per-use basis.

The digital manager

Many view the current technology-driven transformation of the workplace as more significant than the industrial revolution. Being a manager in the digital age can mean that the rules are being rewritten even before a manager has had time to absorb them. The new reality is that a manager has to be open to change, prepared to give up traditional models and eager to embrace new ideas. This can be tough, and keeping the organization's goals in mind is vital.

Once it was enough to know 'what' and 'why' – now technology connects ideas and people, it is more about knowing 'why' and 'who'. This requires a manager to rethink his role: rather than seeing himself as a position in a company hierarchy with a span of control, he should view himself as the centre of a network of flexible internal and external resources, a position from which he can facilitate results and influence outcomes. Technology must be viewed in terms of benefits rather than features: as a way of managing information and enabling collaboration.

Finance

A successful manager need not be an accounting wizard, but she does have to understand the basics of business finance. From the outset, her objectives are likely to have some financial element – she must be knowledgeable and involved in the annual budgeting process, ensuring that she can secure the right resources to achieve her objectives. Understanding and interpreting financial information in various formats is vital to making informed decisions and effectively measuring progress towards her objectives.

Managers are likely to make a better contribution to the organization if they are financially savvy, even though they may rely on the accounting experts to do the hard number-crunching. Finance directors often move on to become chief executives because profit maximization is so important in business. Even a manager in a not-for-profit organization needs some financial skills, because the organization has to manage its limited revenue well and remain solvent.

Finance fundamentals

Most national laws require that profit-making business and regulated charities produce two standard financial statements – the profit-and-loss account and the balance sheet. Managers need to be able to understand these essential documents.

A profit-and-loss account ('P&L'), or income statement, records the inflow of revenue and outflow of expenses over a given period of time, usually annually, and is a vital indicator of an organization's health. A typical P&L shows revenue (turnover) from which costs (such as materials, staff and overheads) are deducted to leave *gross* profit. Additional costs, such as taxation, are then deducted to leave the total *net* profit or loss. The balance sheet is a snapshot of the organization's financial position at a specific date. It shows what is owned (total assets), including cash, inventory and property, balanced against an equal sum of what the company owes (liabilities) and the remaining portion – the owners' or shareholders' equity.

in account

with

MINSTER

BANK L

MACCL

By

1928
Apr 18
May 3

2

Turnover and profit

The money that a business is paid for its products or services by its customers is its turnover or revenue. Profit is the money that is left after all costs and expenses have been paid. Gross profit is the money remaining after the costs of manufacturing the product or delivering the service, plus all indirect costs such as fixed overheads (e.g. office space), have been deducted while net profit is the amount remaining after tax. Think of turnover as the top line: all the money coming into the business. And think of profit as the bottom line: the money that is the last line on the income or profit-and-loss statement.

It is important to be clear about the difference between turnover and profit. A rising turnover indicates an increase in sales, but profit is the real indicator of the success of the business. A business may get a large number of orders but have to pay an agency a high premium for extra staff, so the additional costs might exceed the amount of money earned.

Cash

Cash – currency that is immediately accessible even if not actually in the form of banknotes and coins – comes into a business through sales of goods or services and goes out to pay for costs such as raw materials, wages and office or factory space. The difference between the inflow and outflow of cash is called the net cash flow. A positive cash flow occurs when a business receives more money than it is spending, while a negative cash flow sees it receive less money than it is spending.

As the old saying goes, cash is king. A business may have high turnover and low costs, but if cash is not coming in on a regular basis, perhaps due to late payment from customers, negative cash flow can occur. Any business needs cash to pay its own bills, including rent and wages, and cash allows more flexibility when making business decisions. Managers need to keep an eye on cash; a rule of thumb is to keep enough to cover three months' worth of costs. Many firms produce a cash flow statement, and the cash in a business is shown on the balance sheet.

Costs and overheads

There are two types of costs: fixed costs, also referred to as overheads or indirect costs, and variable or direct costs. Fixed costs remain the same no matter what business activities occur – whether a company sells 1 or 1,000 items. They include rent, bills such as electricity, and wages for permanent staff. Variable costs are directly related to production, rising as production increases and falling as it decreases. For example, a company that makes dresses has the fixed costs of factory and wages but the variable costs of fabric and packaging for each dress. Fixed and variable costs together make up total costs.

It is important for a manager to know all costs and distinguish between the two types of costs. A business aims to make a profit, but it must at least break even (when its revenue and total costs are equal). Managing costs is likely to be a key part of every manager's role, and increasingly firms are looking for creative ways to cut costs by outsourcing, squeezing suppliers or going paperless.

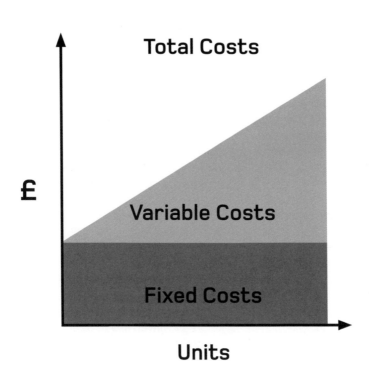

Forecasts

Forecasting is important in any business. Managers have to look ahead in order to create a plan that may include the quantity of raw materials to order, how many people to employ in the coming year or when new products are best launched. This is not about a manager simply putting a finger to the wind – a forecast is typically based on information about the market rather than just on past performance data.

Forecasting in an organization can take place at different levels. A firm may look at what might happen across an entire market or a region where a product is sold; this is a macroeconomic forecast. It may drill down to an industry sales forecast for its type of products. And it may look at its expected sales, taking into account its market share and typically those of its competitors. Many firms look at different scenarios to establish the most likely outcome. Managers involved in sales forecasting always need to be realistic rather than optimistic, as budgets and targets will be based on their figures.

Scenarios and assumptions

Scenario planning is a way for organizations to make long-term plans when there are a number of variables. The power of scenario planning for business was originally established by the oil company Royal Dutch Shell in the 1970s.

Planning for varied scenarios cannot remove uncertainty, but does help avoid total surprises. Different tools can be used, from a simple two-by-two matrix (where there are just two variables), to more complex spreadsheets of 'what if?' scenarios that include numerous interdependent variables and their probabilities. The rule of thumb is to develop at least four scenarios to get a broad range of outcomes beyond just optimistic or pessimistic extremes. Some variables may be more predictable if they are based on past data such as demographic trends. Others, such as economic or political environments, are harder to foresee. Assumptions have to be clearly stated in any scenario; for example, one scenario might assume interest rates of 2 per cent and another 5 per cent, altering their outcomes.

Budgets

Budgeting is the basis for all financial planning: it is an estimate of the money coming into and going out of a business over a specified period of time. The actual money flowing into and out of the organization can then be compared on a regular basis against budget figures to highlight any variances. Adjustments can be made to the budget according to the goals of the business, and as circumstances change. Actual money against budget can be in surplus where a profit is anticipated, balanced if income is expected to equal costs, or in deficit where costs exceed income. The latter is rare unless an organization has access to significant borrowing.

Managers typically get involved in setting their own budgets, and this may involve negotiation with a more senior manager. Once the budget is agreed, managing it is one of the key ways in which finances are controlled in a business. A manager will be expected to take remedial action, for example, if costs appear to be above budget or revenue below budget.

KPIs

Key performance indicators (KPIs) are defined and set to help an organization measure progress toward its goals. They are just as important in not-for-profit organizations as they are in a commercial business.

What gets measured gets done: KPIs are a small number of vital metrics that managers together agree best indicate the organization's success. They need to be relevant, measurable and actionable, and could be anything from the rate of customer returns to a retailer, to the number of agency staff used in a residential care home. The data must be readily available and easily compiled. Together, KPIs give a snapshot of the organization's progress towards its goals: good managers ensure that team members understand their significance. They should be reviewed regularly to assess the results, any action needed and whether the right things are still being measured. Many organizations create and publish a dashboard of KPIs to motivate people and help drive performance.

Cost-benefit analysis

Cost-benefit analysis (CBA) is a way of making simple financial decisions. French engineer Jules Dupuit is generally credited with introducing the concept in the 19th century, whereby the costs of a course of action are compared to its benefits. More complex approaches are commonly used for business-critical decisions, but the basic process is as follows:

- All the costs are considered and estimated – not just manpower, but training required and tools over the lifetime of the project
- All the benefits are considered and assigned a monetary value – includes estimated revenues, time saved, improved customer service, faster travel times and intangible items that will inevitably have a subjective value
- The value of the costs is compared against the value of the benefits to determine the course of action. It may be clear immediately that the benefits outweigh the costs. If not, a pay-back period is often calculated to establish how long it would take to repay the costs.

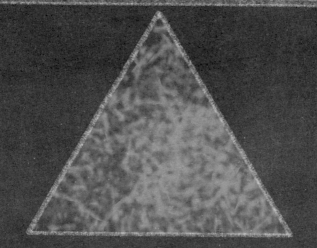

Return on investment

Return on investment (ROI) is one of most commonly used approaches for evaluating the financial consequences of business investments, decisions or actions. It is not enough for a manager to be able to build in a profit margin on the product or service managed – he has to be able to make basic decisions between different courses of action. Being able to work out the ROI enables a comparison: the investment with the highest ROI is the one that should be chosen.

Suppose a marketing manager has to choose between launching two different products. She would compare the ROI for both products by considering everything required for the marketing investment and estimating the potential future sales. To ensure a more realistic figure, a discount rate may be applied to the future revenue because this is worth a different amount than if that revenue were earned today. This is the 'net present value' (NPV), which allows the business to compare the future revenue to alternative investments today.

$$\frac{\left(\begin{array}{c}\text{Gains from investment} \\ - \text{ Cost of Investment}\end{array}\right)}{\text{Cost of Investment}}$$

Glossary

Chain of command
Sequence of how authority and direction flows down from senior management to every level in the organization.

Comfort zone
A situation where employees feel at ease and make little effort.

Competitive advantage
Lead over competitors because of greater value, lower prices or perceived benefits by the customer, enabled through superior design, productivity or process efficiency.

Crisis management
A rigorous approach taken by an organization to deal with an unexpected, potentially threatening incident and minimize repercussions.

Ergonomics
The study of people's working environment and interactions, considering efficiency, safety and well-being.

eBusiness
Electronic business: using the internet to conduct business, manage processes or enable businesses to link together.

eCommerce
Electronic commerce: buying and selling product and services over the internet.

Entrepreneur
An individual who identifies opportunities and often takes risks to start a business.

Flexible working
An approach where employees work an agreed number of hours each week or month, but determine their exact working hours themselves.

Governance
A framework of principles, rules and practices, including a board of directors, that ensures an organization conducts its operations fairly, ethically and legally, and deals with all stakeholders appropriately.

Lean production
A systemic approach to manufacturing from Japan, that focuses on cutting out waste while ensuring quality.

Limited company
A company with a separate legal identity from its shareholders, who have limited liability. It can be privately owned as in a small business, or public, where there are external shareholders.

FMCG
Fast moving consumer goods: products that are regularly purchased at relatively low cost, such as processed foods.

IP
Intellectual property: something unique that a company creates, such as a new product, which can be protected by copyright, patents or trademarks.

Knowledge worker
An employee using their intellect and experience to work with information, rather than to perform manual tasks – often the source of competitive advantage.

Learning curve
The rate at which a person learns new skills; a steep learning curve indicates fast learning and a shallow one shows slow progress.

NGO
Non-governmental organization: an organization that is neither part of government nor a conventional business, set up for a particular purpose, such as campaigning.

Psychological contract
An unwritten understanding between an employee and employer about what each side expects out of the employment relationship.

Real time
Data that is always up-to-date because it is input and processed immediately by a computer system.

Silos

Narrow, vertical, informal structures in organizations where information and activities are retained rather than shared.

Social enterprise

An organization that trades for a social, environmental or community purpose, such as to develop skills in a community. Money is made by trading on an open market but profits are reinvested.

Third sector

Voluntary, non-profit part of economy comprising non-governmental and non-profit organizations including charities, cooperatives and social enterprises.

Time and motion study

A methodical analysis of the specific steps in a task, used to improve employee productivity and efficiency.

Trade-off

A situation involving compromise; balancing two or more opposing issues so that the choice involves a gain in one aspect but a loss in another area.

Triple bottom line

Aiming to measure not just the bottom line of a profit and loss account but the financial, social and environmental performance of an organization over a period of time.

Index

First published in Great Britain
in 2015 by

Quercus
Carmelite House
50 Victoria Embankment
London EC4Y 0DZ

An Hachette UK company

First published in 2015

Paperback ISBN 9781784293260
Ebook ISBN 9781784294496

10 9 8 7 6 5 4 3

Printed and bound in China